Celebrate!

The History and Folklore of Holidays in Nova Scotia

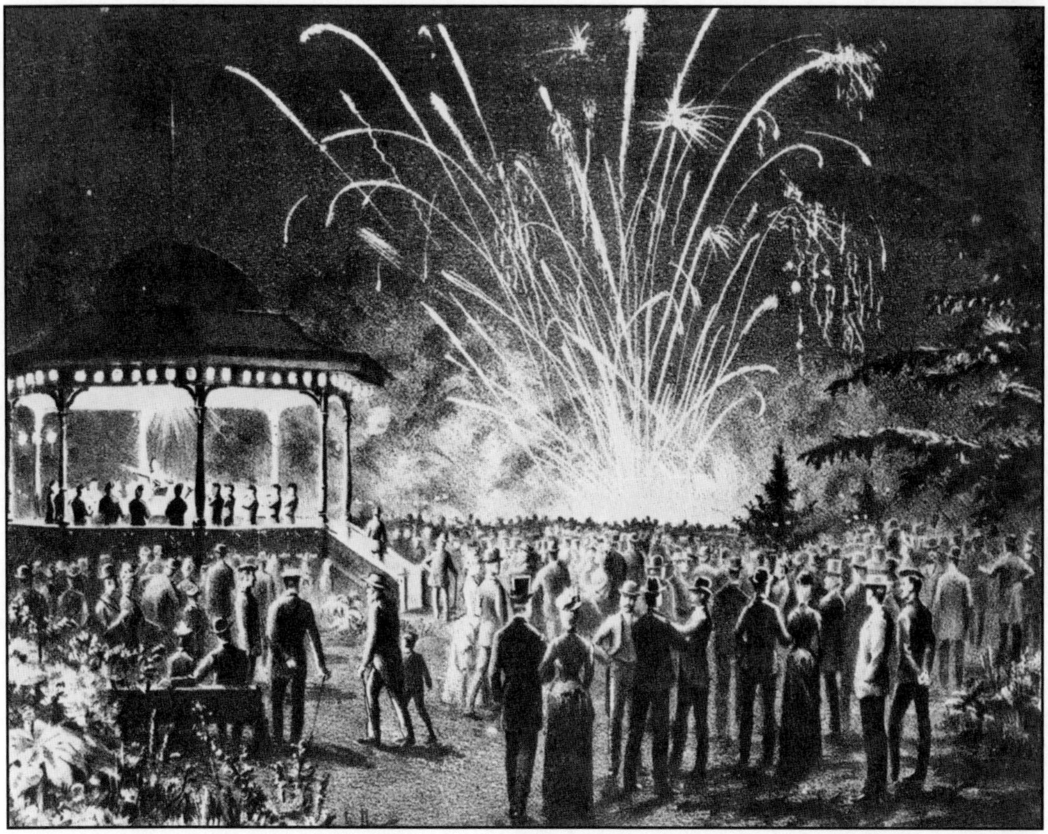

Clary Croft

A Note on Spelling. In accordance with the style used by The Confederacy of Mainland Mi'kmaq, this book uses the following spellings: "Mi'kmaw" when used as an adjective (regardless of whether the noun it modifies is singular or plural) and "Mi'kmaq" when used as a noun to refer to more than one Mi'kmaw person or the nation.

Nimbus Publishing Limited
PO Box 9166
Halifax, NS
B3K 5M8 (902) 455-4286

Printed and bound in Canada
Design: Kathy Kaulbach, Paragon Design Group
Front cover: Fireworks image (background), David Grandy
Title page: Nova Scotia Archives and Records Management
Author photo back cover: Sharon Croft

National Library of Canada Cataloguing in Publication Data
Croft, Clary
Celebrate! : the history and folklore of holidays in Nova Scotia / Clary Croft.
ISBN 1-55109-411-8
1. Holidays—Nova Scotia—Folklore. I. Title.

GT4813.A3N68 2002 394.269716 C2002-903462-0

Canada

The Canada Council for the Arts | Le Conseil des Arts du Canada

We acknowledge the financial support of the Government of Canada through the Book Publishing Industry Development Program (BPIDP) and the Canada Council for our publishing activities.

TABLE OF CONTENTS

ACKNOWLEDGEMENTS

I WOULD LIKE TO THANK the many people who offered me an insight into their personal traditions. I have squirreled away their comments and observations for many years—no doubt they will recognize themselves in these pages.

Thanks to the staff at Nimbus Publishing for their encouragement and interest in this project.

The staff at the Dartmouth Heritage Museum and the Nova Scotia Archives and Records Management (formerly the Public Archives of Nova Scotia) have, yet again, proved their incredible ability to steer me in the right direction and offer advice. It continues to be a pleasure and a privilege to work with the staffs of these institutions.

Many of the traditions mentioned here were touched upon in my regular radio shows for CBC, *Mainstreet*. My thanks to the loyal listeners, the staff on that show, and to my long-time (and now retired) colleague, George Jordan.

Finally—but of paramount importance—my family and friends. My mom, Olive, and dad, Clarence, brother Steve and sisters Carol, Nancy, Sheila, and Carrie have provided me with irreplaceable memories of celebrations. My in-laws, Marjorie and Don Campagna, and my extended family have built a rich extension to my own holiday traditions. My dear friends, Karen and Rodger Middleton, have helped me celebrate the beginning of every New Year for decades.

But most of all, my enduring love and gratitude to my darling wife Sharon, who makes every day a celebration.

INTRODUCTION

When I began work on this book and told people I was gathering material relating to holidays, many thought I would be writing about travels and leisure time. That may come, but this book is about the other kind of holidays—the celebrated events that are determined by specific dates or seasons. Because these events fall on or around dates fixed on a calendar, folklorists refer to them as calendar customs. These calendar customs are often grouped into three categories: religious, patriotic and folk. Easter and Ramadan are examples of Christian and Islamic religious observances; Remembrance Day and Flag Day certainly fall into the patriotic category; and Valentine's Day is a good example of a folk holiday.

Certain holidays are referred to as "moveable events." That is to say, they don't fall on a specific date, but are determined by the solar or lunar configurations for marking time. Celebrants need to consult their specific calendars to find exact dates for holidays such as Easter, Hanukkah, and the Chinese New Year. Other holidays, such as Canada Day, are statutory—created and regulated by a government body.

Holidays are kept alive in many ways. Groundhog Day is not independently celebrated or marked in any major way by the general populace. It is really only promoted by the popular press and by special interest groups who promote their area's soothsaying rodent as a form of bragging right or tourist attraction. Religions have very specific codified rites surrounding holidays. These are almost always modified and added to with folk beliefs. The majority of the world's Christians celebrate Christmas on December 25, but the folk traditions surrounding this celebration are as varied as the participants.

The interesting thing about our celebrations is just that—they are "our" celebrations! The way you celebrate is, in your mind at least, the correct way. Just try to change a tradition in your family. We like to think of ourselves as progressive—moving with the times. That works for many things, but not celebrations. Many a relationship has been strained by merging one family's traditions with another. Fortunately, in the end, a compromise is most often reached and a new form of merged tradition evolves which will, itself, become a new tradition. That's how folklore works!

The holidays celebrated in Nova Scotia are prime examples of how these merging of folk traditions and calendar customs have evolved over centuries. Canada has a strong adherence to the concept of multiculturalism, where cultures remain intact while co-existing with others. But, the truth is, our folk beliefs are frequently blended with the beliefs of other cultural and racial groups. In an article titled "Ethnic Identity in Nova Scotia," my friend Dr. Jim Morrison from Saint Mary's University in Halifax writes: "We live in a multicultural society that is also a plural society. By this I mean that no ethnic group has successfully remained aloof from all others for more than a generation."

I can attest to that statement from my own experience. When I married Sharon Campagna in 1972 I brought my traditions based upon German, Irish, Scots, and Iberian origins and blended them with her

Acadian and British customs. For over thirty years we have been blending and reinventing our own traditions. Some of each family's traditions have been put aside, and some of the new ones we invented may be carried on by others in our family. Only time and an exhaustive folkloric investigative study (read tongue in cheek) will tell. If the rituals we celebrate are not important enough to others, they will be lost. One can never be sure what will survive. What we can be sure of is the diverse and varied ways in which holidays continue to be celebrated in Nova Scotia.

With the introduction and assimilation of the Catholic faith into Mi'kmaw culture, which had its own highly developed celebratory rites, new traditions and beliefs were adopted or integrated. As other distinct ethnic and cultural groups came to Nova Scotia, they worked to make the traditional celebrations from their homelands a vital part of their daily lives. In fact, this arrival of various groups helped have cultural and ethnic holidays added to the list of religious holidays acknowledged by the government. But it was custom that caused the specific holidays to survive.

The celebration of rites and customs in isolation has made it difficult for those traditions to become popular holidays. The Baha'i calendar custom of Naw-Rúz (a celebration of regrowth and renewal) has been regularly celebrated by Nova Scotian adherents to the faith since 1938. But because it is not well known outside the Baha'i community, Naw-Rúz isn't considered a "popular folk custom" of the region. In fact, I had never heard of it until I began researching this book. St. Patrick's Day, on the other hand, is celebrated or at least acknowledged by almost all non-Irish peoples in the province.

Because people of many different ethnicities and religions live side by side in Nova Scotia, it is only natural that we should come into contact with the beliefs of others. Over a two-day period in May of this year (2002), I saw two examples of this inter-cultural contact: a sign in the window of a Bedford store advising their customers that they would be closed in observance of a Baha'i holiday, and a vendor at the Halifax city market selling Beltane smudge sticks. I also noted that both occurrences were different enough from the mainstream to warrant comments from observers. Some expressed interest, some were curious, some were indifferent, but most recognized that these materials were not the norm. I expect that in a few years, holidays and materials like these will be commonplace.

A great number of celebrations or festivals deal with ethnicity. While many move beyond the specific interests of their immediate celebration, it is precisely because they are specific that they survive. Nova Scotians of German heritage have introduced the more inclusive celebration of Oktoberfest. African Nova Scotians have taken the month of February to celebrate Black History Month (also called African Heritage Month). People with origins in France and the British Isles often have celebrations on the days acknowledging the patron saints of their individual countries—St. Andrew's Day for Scotland or St. David's Day for Wales, for example. When you consider that there are close to one hundred different ethnic groups in the province, the list of holidays celebrated by specific interest cultural groups is immense. Add to that list the various religious and national holidays and days set aside for special events, such as Gay Pride Day, and the list grows even longer.

In fact, Canada will soon celebrate a new national holiday. On April 24, 2002, Liberal Member of Parliament David Pratt moved "that in the opinion of this House, the government should, on an annual basis, proclaim the first Sunday in June 'Canadian Forces Day' in recognition of the tremendous contribution by the Canadian Forces, both at home and abroad, in such areas as the defense of Canada, our NATO commitments, humanitarian assistance, disaster relief, search and rescue and peacekeeping." After much debate, a revised motion passed unanimously.

Only time will tell how well Canadian Forces Day is observed, celebrated and acknowledged. Three weeks after the holiday was proclaimed by parliament, the military public relations offices in Halifax and Ottawa told me they were working on plans to celebrate the day, but as yet had made no decisions.

Time, and the sentiments of Canadians, will decide whether the holiday will last. We've seen holidays come and go, and we will continue to see them evolve.

We didn't always have the same holidays we have today. Just look at the list of holidays from *Belcher's Almanac*, published in Halifax for 1870, which begins by informing the reader that the almanac takes in the entire province:

> *Calculated for Halifax...and for ordinary purposes will serve, with sufficient accuracy, for all parts of the Province, including the Island of Cape Breton...Fixed and Moveable Feasts, Anniversaries, etc. those marked thus * Dominion Holidays, by how, in the Dominion, as also any day appointed by Proclamation for a general fast or thanksgiving.*

*Circumcision .... January 1
*Epiphany .... January 6
Prince Albert Victor of Wales b. 1864 .... January 8
Princess Royal, m. 1858 .... January 25
Queen Victoria, m. 1840 .... February 10
Septuagesima (third Sunday before Lent) February 13
Sexagesima (second Sunday before Lent) February 20
Princess Louisa of Wales, b. 1867 .... February 20
Quing, or Shrove Sunday .... February 27
St. David .... March 1
*Ash Wednesday .... March 2
Prince of Wales, m. 1863 .... March 10
St. Patrick .... March 17
Princess Louisa, b. 1848 .... March 18
Annunciation - Lady Day .... March 25
Duke Cambridge, b. 1819 .... March 26
Prince Leopold, b. 1853 .... April 7
Palm Sunday .... April 10
Princess Beatrice, b. 1857 .... April 14
*Good Friday .... April 15
Easter Sunday .... April 17
*Easter Monday .... April 18
Napoleon III, b. 1808 .... April 20
St. George .... April 23
Princess Alice, b. 1843 .... April 25
Prince Arthur, b. 1850 .... May 1
Rogation (day of prayer for harvest) Sunday May 22
*Queen Victoria, b. 1819 .... May 24
Princess Helena, b. 1846 .... May 25
*Ascension Day .... May 26
Holy Thursday .... May 26
Prince George of Wales, b. 1865 .... June 3
Whit Sunday - Pentecost .... June 5
Trinity Sunday .... June 12

*Corpus Christi	June 16
Accession Queen Victoria, 1837	June 20
Settlement of Halifax, 1749	June 21
St. John Baptist	June 24
Midsummer Day	June 24
*St. Peter and St. Paul	June 29
Anniversary Dominion of Canada	July 1
Princess Alice, m. 1862	July 1
Princess Helena, m. 1866	July 5
Prince of Wales visit to Halifax, 1860	July 29
Lammas Day	August 1
Prince Alfred, b. 1844	August 6
St. Michael	September 29
Michaelmas Day	September 29
All-Hallows Eve	October 31
*All Saints	November 1
All Souls	November 2
Prince of Wales, b. 1841	November 9
Princess Royal, b. 1840	November 21
Advent Sunday	November 27
St. Andrew	November 30
Princess Alexandra, b. 1844	December 1
*Conception Blessed Virgin Mary	December 14
Prince Consort died, 1842	December 14
St. Thomas	December 21
*Christmas Day	December 25
St. Stephen	December 26
St. John Evangelist	December 27
Innocents	December 28

It's amazing how much our present list of holidays differs from the 1870 edition of the *Belcher's Almanac*. Twenty-five years later, the same publication omitted most of the royal dates except Queen Victoria's birthday and that of the Prince of Wales. But, by then, they were acknowledging other religions and cultures by adding non-Western celebrations:

> *"The year 5650 of the Jewish Era begins on September 19, 1895.*
> *Ramadan (month of abstinence observed by the Turks) commences February 26, 1895.*
> *The year of the Mohammedan Era begins on June 24, 1895."*

Sometimes interest in particular holidays wanes, at other times the holidays go out of fashion altogether. During the 1800s, major holidays in Nova Scotia used to be celebrated on the saints' days—St. George, St. Andrew, and St. Patrick. These days were marked by parades, speeches, and lavish dinners with numerous toasts. Most public buildings were closed.

The Battle of Waterloo was fought in 1815, but as late as the 1840s Waterloo Day was celebrated in Halifax by the general citizenry and the veterans of the decisive battle that defeated Napoleon. A day in June was set aside for reviewing troops on the Commons and for mock battles held by the Waterloo veterans. But once the veterans died the celebration followed. The day was lost, not literally, but the celebration was no longer relevant to the living.

However, there could be no fear that a day would go by without some kind of celebration. There will always only be 365 days in the Western calendar (366 in a leap year) but each day has dozens of holidays ascribed to it. Some fall on specific days; others are determined by the sun and/or the moon. Governments can decree that certain holidays be moved from their traditional dates to accommodate people who want to have more time off from work, or to make a long weekend out of the celebration. Victoria Day, May 24, is always celebrated on a Monday even though the actual date falls on that day only once in every seven years.

The dates I use in this book are those associated with the Gregorian calendar, but because of the "lost eleven days of 1752," items dated before 1752 should not always be transposed into contemporary dates.

Beginning in 1582, most of Western society gradually moved from the Julian to the Gregorian calendar. But, like most human contrivances for registering the passage of time, the system is not without its flaws. The Gregorian calendar is approximately 0.0003 points of a day (about 26 seconds) longer than the average solar year. So, every 3,323 years we gain a complete day. Eventually we have to eliminate some of these calendar days to get in line with the solar time reference. In 1751, the government in England decided to officially adopt the Gregorian system and, at the same time, play catch up by removing eleven days from the next calendar year—1752. While it was just a reshuffling of numbers, many people were outraged. There were riots in the streets of Britain, with people crying, "Give us back our eleven days!"

The government listened, they noted the displeasure of the populace, and proceeded with the planned change. So, in September of 1752, Wednesday the second was followed by Thursday the fourteenth. The government also took the opportunity to officially recognize the first of January as New Year's Day, which until that time had been held on March 25. This fact explains why many of our financial and business institutions close their business year at the end of March.

Halifax had been founded three years earlier but it already had a newspaper. How did it report the loss of eleven days?

The *Halifax Gazette* for September 16, 1752, has survived, but with no mention of the change of date. Naturally the dates between the third of September and the thirteenth are missing—they never happened. What the paper did deem important for their readers was an announcement that not enough tickets were sold to raise funds for a lighthouse, so ticket buyers would be given back their money. By the end of the month, when one would expect some coverage of any civic unrest associated with the lost eleven days, the paper was silent. The big news in the *Halifax Gazette* came from the American colonies concerning the "electrical experiments perform[ed] by our most consummate naturalist ... Mr. Franklin in Philadelphia."

Maybe it was the beginning of Canadianism: we either didn't care about the lost days or were too polite to say anything about it! At least there were no major holidays taken out of the eleven-day change to the calendar—then we might have seen riots in the streets.

Holidays are constantly evolving—and that's what this book is all about. I've chosen only those holidays that are celebrated by the majority of the people living in Nova Scotia, or holidays that are significant to a major traditional cultural group and that have a history long enough for traditions and beliefs to change, evolve, and enter into mainstream society. I've included several holidays that were, at one time, considered important events in the province, but have since gone out of favour or had their popularity wane. These days are examples of how a tradition can become lost if it isn't moved forward by those celebrating it. While certain ethnic and cultural groups have been celebrating their holiday traditions for centuries in Nova Scotia, those traditions have, for the most part, remained particular to that group. They are important elements overall in traditional folk culture and I hope future collectors will concentrate on the non-Western cultural and religious groups that continue to add to our province's rich folklore. In the interim, I have given brief overviews of those cultural groups and some of their major holiday celebrations in the appendix.

For this book, I've included examples gleaned from folklore and cultural collectors as well as material from research I've conducted myself over the past thirty years. The material therefore is biased to a Western perspective.

For those readers who will be sparked to recall their own traditions, you'll find several pages in the back of the book for you to add your own material. Its like beginning a folklore journal with a little kick-start from me. But for now I hope you enjoy the stories of our holidays' origins. I've included some background and, where possible, a direct Nova Scotian perspective. Many superstitions and beliefs surround holidays. I've included quite a few from the folklore collections of Arthur Fauset, Helen Creighton, Marion Robertson, and others. When the item is common and collected from several sources, no name will follow, but when specific, the collector's name will appear in brackets after the belief.

Helen Creighton collecting folklore from Norman McGrath, Victoria Beach, 1947.

JANUARY

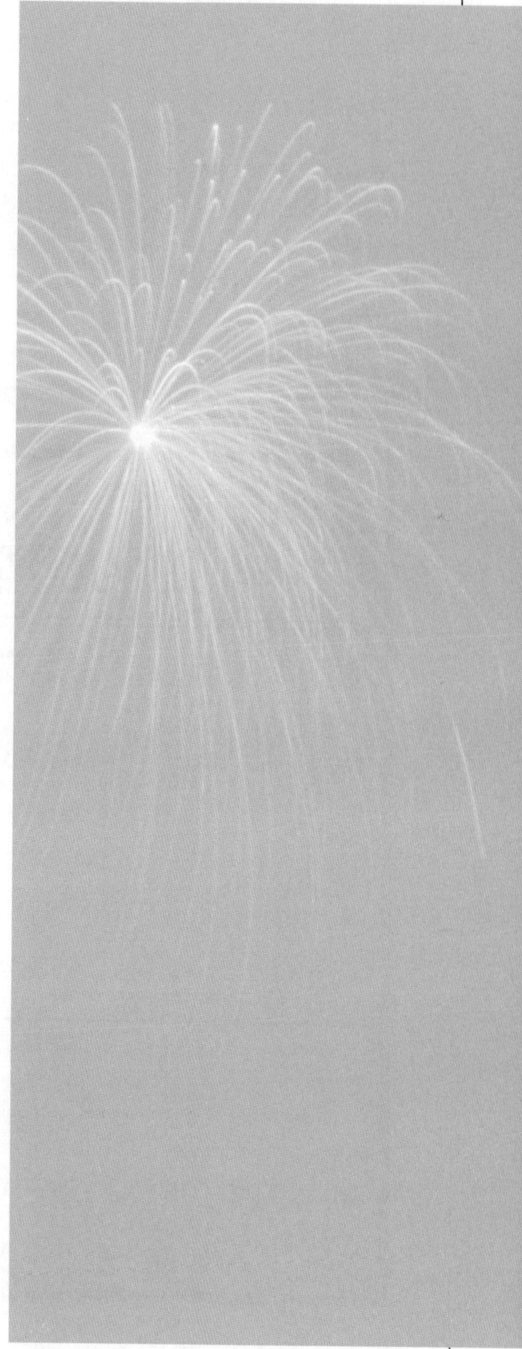

NEW YEAR'S DAY

JANUARY 1

THE FIRST DAY OF THE NEW CALENDAR YEAR is the most widely celebrated holiday in the world. But not everyone celebrates the new year on January 1. Jews celebrate Yom Kippur close to the autumn equinox. Some Hindus celebrate the first day of each season, so they have four New Year's Days. In Japan, the first day of January is called *gantan*, but "*shogatsu*," the New Year's holiday, starts on the first and lasts officially until the fourth but in reality usually until the seventh or eighth. In Mexico, February 2 corresponds to the Aztec new year festivities, while in Sierra Leone the Mintage people celebrate the new year in late April or early May at corn-sowing time.

Whatever date is chosen to celebrate the new year, there are some customs that are common to everyone—many involving food. It's common for celebrants to share and eat new food, wear new clothes, and begin the year with all debts settled and all conflicts with others resolved. Obviously, some customs are easier to carry out than others!

The ancient Babylonians were among the first to introduce the ever-popular but rarely kept New Year's resolution. We know from early Babylonian writings that one of their most popular resolutions was the act of returning borrowed farm tools.

One of the most interesting New Year's customs I remember from my childhood is beginning a weather calendar. My mother still keeps one every year. It works like this: you record the weather for the first twelve days of January on the calendar. These are known as leading days. The weather conditions for

SOME NEW YEAR RESOLUTIONS

RESOLVED That Royal Purple Laying Meal is the Proper food for Hens to insure a better supply of the popular 75c. eggs.

also

RESOLVED That Royal Purple Calf Meal will induce young stock and pigs to put on flesh more quickly and cheaper than any other food.

also

RESOLVED That National Light American Kerosene Oil is cleaner and more economical than any other oil for heaters and lamps.

also

RESOLVED That we will buy all of the above from the Quality Hardware Store.

If you act on these suggestions you are in a fair way to be Prosperous and Happy.

Yours with Best Wishes for a Happy New Year

KARL FREEMAN
Proprietor
BRIDGETOWN, N. S.

Advertisement for New Year's resolution with chicken feed and fuel oil from Karl Freeman, Bridgetown

each of the twelve leading days is supposed to forecast the kind of weather one can expect for the corresponding month. So, if January 1 is stormy, you can expect a stormy January; if January 7 is a sunny day, July will be sunny and dry. I've never conducted a survey on the accuracy of this approach to weather forecasting—it might spoil the fun!

The Nova Scotian version of "first footing" is derived from the Scottish tradition of ensuring good luck in the new year by not allowing anyone but a dark-complexioned or dark-haired male to cross the threshold first on January 1. In some communities in Nova Scotia such men were recruited to go from door to door early New Year's Day morning so the local inhabitants would be sure to have good luck. In other circumstances, incentives were offered to ensure the presence of a dark male at the door on the morn of January 1. In *The Chestnut Pipe: Folklore of Shelburne County*, Marion Robertson cites the story of one family who always offered a jackknife to the first dark boy who came to the door on New Year's Day. Apparently, when they opened the door to their first visitor of the day, without fail a boy would be waiting in the cold to be the "first footer" and claim his token.

Shelburne played host to another New Year's Day custom—the Santa Anna Brigade, a ceremonial parade of young men, who went about town playing horns and beating drums. This was not an isolated custom; describing a New Glasgow New Year's morning in 1866, Annie Brown wrote: "a procession of people called The Horribles trotted through town. They are the boys of the town, dressed up to look ridiculous and ugly as possible, and they drive or ride round making noises on pipes and things. We rushed down to see them after breakfast, and then got a big three-seated sleigh and drove all round the town several times. In the afternoon of course, we did not go out, but received the callers, which were thirty-seven."

Visiting and receiving New Year's Day callers was a common form of entertainment in the eighteenth and nineteenth centuries. In Cape Breton it was the

On the eve of the first new moon, hold a mirror and walk backwards towards salt water. Your sweetheart's face will show in the mirror (Fauset).

Have money in the house on New Year's Day and you will have wealth throughout the year.
If you sew on New Year's Day, you'll sew for the rest of the year (Creighton).

It's bad luck to hang a calendar before New Year's Day.

If the first foot is a woman
And that woman is fair
In all the days that follow
You will have a care.
(old Cape Breton rhyme)

custom to take a gift to the hostess: a lump of coal or sugar, a sheaf of wheat, or a penny—something to represent abundance and prosperity for the coming year. Remember, in nineteenth century Nova Scotia, coal meant warmth! Another popular gift (and one said to ensure a different kind of warmth) was whiskey or rum. Receiving callers and enjoying treats of liquor are still important parts of the ritual of the New Year's Day levee.

The origins of contemporary levees are found in the special morning assembly held in France at the court of King Louis XIV. It was considered a great honour to be in attendance when the king was getting up in the morning to begin his day—his "levée." Of course, it was a male-only event.

Levees, as we have come to know them, developed in the eighteenth century and were held on many different occasions, not just New Year's Day. In Halifax, during the 1770s, royal birthdays and public holidays were almost always celebrated with a levee at Government House. The participants not only got a drink but were treated to the trooping of soldiers on the Grand Parade, perhaps followed in the evening by a ball. In fact, levees became so frequent that Lord Dalhousie, the lieutenant-governor of Nova Scotia from 1816 to 1820 wrote, "held a levee as is usual on New Year's Day. A most ridiculous ceremony and troublesome from the frequency of them."

While year-round levees might have become troublesome and annoyingly frequent for officials and the vice royals, the traditional New Year's levee continued to grow in popularity into the nineteenth century

Happy New Year, 1909 postcard, sent to Mrs. George H. Potter, Bear River.

when it reached its zenith. The events provided a golden opportunity for men to make the rounds of the community in the morning, then call on ladies in the afternoon. Levees would remain almost entirely the domain of men until World War Two, and, even then, few women attended until the 1960s.

So, how did the early levees differ from those celebrated today? The military and civic leaders held the majority of the levees in the early years of settlement in Nova Scotia. Then, lodges, fraternal organizations, and clubs began adding their own levees. Soon, it took the better part of the morning to make the rounds—and the keen participants began early! They had to. Traditionally, the official visitation aspects of the levees were supposed to be over by noon, which left plenty of time for the gentlemen to begin their afternoon levees by calling on the ladies.

As each man made a call, he was obliged to leave his visiting card. The number of cards a young lady received was duly noted and helped ensure her social status for the year. Hostesses, especially those with unmarried daughters, vied for the greatest number of callers. A Halifax lady described her pleasure at the number of visitors that attended her 1854 levee by writing, "by one o'clock we were all dressed and in the parlour. The first ring was Doctor Delf and after a little while they came pouring in…the whole number through the day was about 140 ."

Not only did the gentlemen have to make the social rounds visiting the ladies, they had to comply with the expectation that they consume enormous quantities of drink—at least one at each stop. At the end of the nineteenth century, Halifax businessman Henry Stairs wrote, "[the] custom was to visit as many ladies as possible and have a drink at each stop. The method was to fix on one liquor…Father used to boast that he made 67 calls in one day on claret but I

New Year ad for Charles Dargie & Sons Ltd., Furniture store, Annapolis Royal

understand that Jimmy Lithgow did better than that by making 71 on scotch whiskey before he had to be carried home. Of course, Jimmy was known for his fondness of the bottle."

Nineteenth-century levees resembled today's pub crawls. During the twentieth century, a move toward more responsible consumption saw hostesses offering alternatives—popular drinks in 1917 were cider and pineapple punch. When Nova Scotians began paying lip service to the concept of prohibition, many hosts claimed to offer coffee. After all, a cup of hot brown coffee could hide the telltale colour of illicit rum very well.

While today's levees are still seen by some as an opportunity to indulge in a bit of the "hair of the dog" after New Year's Eve celebrations, most hosts are offering up alternatives. Refreshments can include beer and spirits, but they will frequently be augmented by sandwiches, consommé, and chowder. But one must always be aware of wolves in sheep's clothing! At a naval levee in Halifax, you might be offered a cup of moosemilk, said to have been invented at the Stadacona Naval Base. I can't imagine any moose calf being nursed on a mixture of cream, rum, brandy, and spices.

Perhaps after downing a few drams of moosemilk, you might be ready to participate in another New Year's Day ritual—the Polar Bear Swim. Disrobing in frigid temperatures and plunging into near freezing waters have become a rite of passage for many celebrants. The act itself, not necessarily associated with a New Year's custom, is common in Scandinavia, where it's seen as a way to improve blood circulation and strengthen the heart.

While our Canadian counterparts on the West Coast may have initiated the custom in this country, it's the hearty residents on the Atlantic coast that deserve respect (or pity). I'd take the temperate waters off Vancouver any day over those of Nova Scotia. In several communities throughout the province, "polar bears" take to the waters either as members of organized clubs, in spontaneous groups of revellers, or as individuals. Depending on the initiative of the polar bear club participants, the weather, and, in some cases, the amplitude of the previous evening's party, the number of people willing to take the dip is variable. In 2001, authorities in Halifax canceled the swim held annually for many years at Black Rock Beach in the city's Point Pleasant Park. The reason: pollution in the harbour. Although a few valiant souls made an appearance for the media, most Halifax-area polar bears joined with a group of hardy souls in Herring Cove, just outside of Halifax Harbour.

While many participants in polar bear swims across the country make a mad dash into the water, there is one custom that separates the genuine polar bear from the wimp. Tradition dictates that a true polar bear must actually swim; some even maintain you have to "get your head wet." This isn't a problem for the folks in Herring Cove. They don't run in from a beach. They don goofy costumes and jump off a wharf. Happy frigid New Years Folks!

We've recently celebrated a milestone new year—

Bank of Felicity note, January 1, 1884. To Mr. and Mrs. Creighton - 366 days of happiness.

one filled with excitement, fear and controversy. The excitement was over the celebration of the second millennium, the fear over what might happen to the world's computer systems, and the controversy over which date the actual millennium falls on. We even coined a new term for the turning point—Y2K. It was the buzzword on everyone's lips, even though few people knew what it meant. While presenting a review of millennium celebrations for CBC Radio's "Mainstreet" program, I did an informal poll to see how many people could tell me what Y2K meant. Less than ten percent had a solid answer. The "Y" was easy—"year." The "2" was obvious—"2000." But few knew that the "K" stood for "kilo," from the Greek meaning one thousand—as in kilometre, or kilobyte, a common enough term for anyone with a modicum of computer savvy.

Since few computer companies had thought far enough ahead to format their systems to handle the changeover from numbering the years starting with "19," they had no idea what would happen to the global infrastructure once the gods of the hard drive were asked to compute 2000 into their standards. Needless to say, it had a lot of people upset—except those selling the updating systems.

There were also those who saw the dawn of the new millennium as either a frightening or much-anticipated event. In a 1997 poll conducted by the Associated Press of America, nearly one quarter of the adult Christians in the United States believed the world would end with the return of Christ in the year 2000.

How did our first millennium counterparts feel about the date turning from 999 to 1000? Did they panic or gather in churches and other sacred places for sanctuary on December 31, 999? It seems not. Since most marked only the passing seasons and few followed any calendar days, except those prescribed by the church, the turn of the century wasn't a big to-do. Apparently, few people even knew the precise date of their own birth. Of course, at that time, the majority of the world's population wasn't following the Western concept of the calendar as we know it today. Millions of Chinese, Jews, and Muslims had their own forms of marking time. For them, December 31, 999 was merely another day, rather than a new millennium or a new century. In fact, people following the

Western method of marking time didn't even use the word "century" as a calendar date until 1626. Before that, "century" denoted a Roman military unit.

By the end of the eighteenth century it seems to have been the arrival of the zeros that had people concerned. Not that they feared zeros—the debate was over which date was the real starting point in the new century.

We saw that debate reach its zenith in the move from the first to second millennium. Was it correct to mark the actual change on January 1, 2000 or January 1, 2001? I personally celebrated with my family and friends in 2000, but I have friends who insisted on celebrating the big event the next year. It was a hot debate, and certainly not a new one. On January 1, 1801, the *Connecticut Current* published this poem:

Precisely at twelve o'clock last night,
The eighteenth century took its flight;
Full many a calculating head,
Has racked its brains, its ink has shed;
To prove by metaphysics fine,
A hundred means but ninety-nine,
While at their wisdom others wondered,
But took one more to make a hundred.

One hundred years later, did Nova Scotians handle the entry into the twentieth century any better than their American neighbours? It seems to have been of little concern if you gauge it by interest in the major provincial newspapers of the day. The *Nova Scotian*, for December 30, 1899, has no mention of a new century, just news of the Fenian scare and the Boer War.

So, the debate over which date is correct for celebrating the genuine new year will probably continue into the third millennium. If Canada and the world survive, the folks living in Cape Spear, Newfoundland, will still be the first to welcome the third millennium. Well, not quite. St. Pierre and Miquelon will actually be first—they are on French time. As I said, it all depends on whose calendar you follow.

EPIPHANY

JANUARY 6

JANUARY 6 HAS FOUR TITLES: Old (or Little) Christmas, Twelfth Night, Epiphany and St. Distaff Day.

When the Western calendar was changed in 1752, eleven days were eliminated from the year. Therefore, for people who still followed the old Julian calendar, January 6 was the traditional birth date of Christ—Old Christmas in the new calendar. Since it falls upon the twelfth day after December 25, January 6 is also traditionally known in Great Britain as Twelfth Night—a name William Shakespeare gave to a play in which the folkloric beliefs of magic and the supernatural associated with the celebration drive the action. The play is said to have first been performed on Twelfth Night. The third title the day bears is Feast of the Epiphany. "Epiphany" means manifestation; the day is meant to mark the twelfth day after Christ's birth, when he was made manifest to the Gentiles by the visit of the Magi. Finally (and in today's society, rarely), January 6 is also called St. Distaff Day to mark the time when women (the so-called distaff side of the sexes) were supposed to return to work at their spinning wheels and other domestic tasks.

In some areas of Nova Scotia special rituals were part of the Epiphany or Old Christmas traditions (see December).

All Christmas decorations must be taken down if you don't want bad luck.

Between Christmas and Epiphany, accept Christmas cake at every house you enter. You will receive a month of happiness for every piece eaten.

MARTIN LUTHER KING, JR. DAY JANUARY

ALTHOUGH NOT AN OFFICIAL Canadian holiday, Martin Luther King, Jr. Day holds special significance for most Nova Scotians of African heritage. And, over the past few years, it has also become a day for all people to mark the peaceful struggle for human rights around the world.

Martin Luther King, Jr. was an American Baptist minister and civil rights advocate. He worked tirelessly throughout his life to gain political and economic freedom for millions of African Americans, through his advocacy of non-violence. A charismatic leader and speaker, his stirring "I have a dream" speech, delivered on the steps of the Lincoln Memorial in Washington, D.C., on August 28, 1963, moved the hearts of a nation and the world. The following year, 1964, he was awarded the Nobel Peace Prize. Tragically, he was assassinated in 1968.

Although Dr. King's actual birthday was on January 17, the holiday to honour his efforts is observed on the third Monday in January. This holiday was signed into law in the United States in 1986 by President Ronald Reagan.

It has become customary for Nova Scotians to acknowledge Dr. King's work on this American holiday with tributes, remembrances, and celebrations of the emancipation of enslaved persons in the British colonies. And while the history of African Canadians is much more than one of enslavement, it is a story that needs to be retold so that tragic part of our history may never be repeated.

Enslaved people were sold in Nova Scotia well into the middle of the eighteenth century. Britain, and her colonies, adopted the Imperial Act in 1833, abolishing slavery throughout the empire. Most historians agree that by the first decade of the nineteenth century, slavery (but not the many forms of indenturing akin to slavery), had vanished in Nova Scotia.

It can hardly be expected that racism and bigotry would be erased with the stroke of a pen. In the August 23, 1833, edition of the *Morning Chronicle*, we find barely a mention of the Imperial Act. The paper does contain a racist article, meant to be humorous, written in pseudo-African Canadian speech between "Cato" and "Cuff," concerning safe foods to eat to avoid cholera. Other items the paper considered of interest included safe wells, military and social news, and the discovery of a raspberry with a circumference of two inches. In small print in the general news section was mention that the slavery opposition bill in Britain's Parliament had been agreed to. Further on was a short article on an unidentified Black reformer's speech in the British Parliament, where he is quoted saying, "they should not judge of the Negro by what they saw of him in slavery; or in savage life." The reformer described favourable conditions in the Caribbean island of St. Domingo, but the paper was quick to note he "was not an advocate of giving compensation to the West India planters."

But the people most affected by the passing of the Imperial Act were, naturally, those who the day before had been enslaved. On the day it became law the congregation of the African Chapel on Cornwallis Street in Halifax, led by Reverend Richard Preston, sang the spiritual:

Sound the loud timbrels o're Egypt's dark sea,
Jehovah hath triumphed his people are free.

BURNS DAY JANUARY 25

SCOTS THROUGHOUT THE WORLD gather in the evening on January 25 to honour their most famous son, Robert Burns, considered by many to be Scotland's greatest bard. He was born on January 25, 1759, and captured (some say romanticized) in verse life in Scotland just before the Industrial Revolution.

Burns was familiar with traditional Scottish folk songs and is credited with writing dozens of popular tunes. But, he was more a collector and adapter. He collected over three hundred folk songs, many published in *Scots Musical Museum*. In fact, his popular song "Comin' Thru the Rye" was adapted from bawdy lyrics he collected from a traditional singer. He edited out the bawdy songs, but kept them for his privately published *The Merry Muse of Caledonia*. His most famous song, and the staple of every New Year's Eve celebration, is "Auld Lang Syne."

Nova Scotia has strong connections with the memory of Burns. Love for his work was a common bond for many people of Scottish heritage in the province. In 1884 the Reverend Robert Grant wrote glowingly of him in a book published in Halifax entitled *Scotia's Immortal Bard*. Grant made no mention of Burns's infidelities and his penchant for bawdy songs, but painted a very saint-like image of the man.

Although Burns Night continues to be celebrated with vigor by Scots in Nova Scotia, it was of paramount importance in the nineteenth and early twentieth centuries. Clan organizations and Scottish ritual societies held annual Burns Night celebrations, and major celebrations were held in Halifax on January 25, 1859, on the centenary of his birth. Parades were

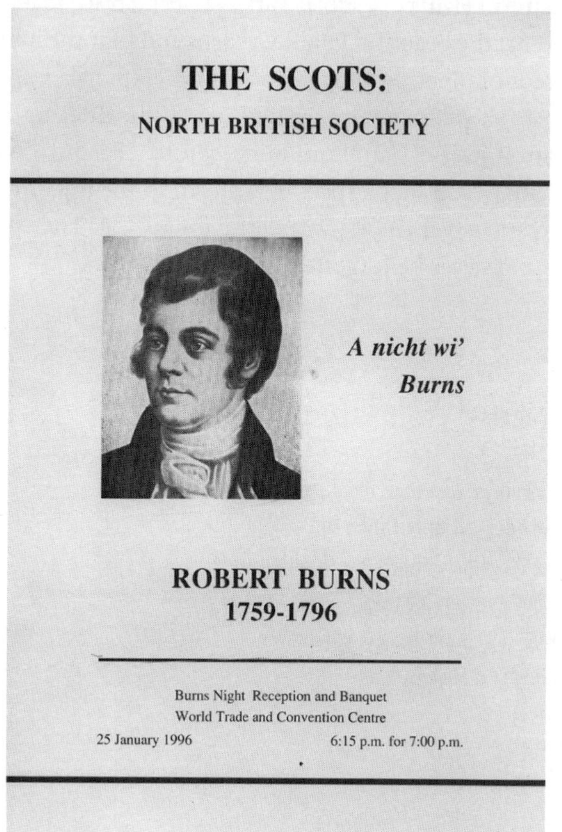

THE SCOTS:

NORTH BRITISH SOCIETY

A nicht wi' Burns

ROBERT BURNS
1759-1796

Burns Night Reception and Banquet
World Trade and Convention Centre
25 January 1996 6:15 p.m. for 7:00 p.m.

The Scots: North British Society, program for Burns Night Reception and Banquet, 1996. The author gave the keynote speech.

held, private and public business closed down, and buildings were draped with banners. At the Temperance Hall, men and women gathered to listen to speeches and readings from the bard's works, followed by a men-only dinner in the evening where a local write-up on the event said, "We believe that this is the first occasion when champagne was dealt out without restraint to all present." Over fifteen toasts were proposed and the festivities ended well after two-thirty in the morning.

In the last century, women began joining the evening dinner, at which traditional Scottish fare was served. Even now, a Burns Night supper will probably include: powsowdie—sheep's head broth; Cabbie-claw—dried cod with horseradish and egg sauce; and haggis—boiled sheep stomach stuffed with minced mutton, oatmeal, and spices. The haggis is given respectful honours, and is eulogized with verse. The piper who escorts the delicacy into the assembly is given a wee dram of whiskey.

But for all the festivities celebrated on Burns Night, and the great expense some people go to dress in Highland regalia, it's ironic that the bard himself died in 1796 at the age of thirty-seven, in poverty and unable to pay his debts. His form is immortalized in a statue in Halifax's Victoria Park—a fitting place to look over at the beautiful Public Gardens and hear the hundreds of pipers leading tourists through the glades. In a prophetic statement written in a 1786 letter to his patron, Gavin Hamilton, Burns wrote, "For my own affairs...you may expect henceforth to see my birthday inscribed among wonderful events." He knew he would never be forgotten.

Address to a Haggis

Fair fa' your honest, sonsie face,
Great Chieftain o' the puddin-race!
Aboon them a' ye tak your place,
Painch, tripe, or thairm:
Weel are ye wordy of a grace
As lang's my arm.

Ye Pow'rs, wha mak mankind your care,
And dish them out their bill o' fare,
Auld Scotland wants nae skinking ware,
That jaups in luggies;
But, if ye wish her gratefu' prayer,
Gie her a Haggis!

by Robert Burns

FEBRUARY

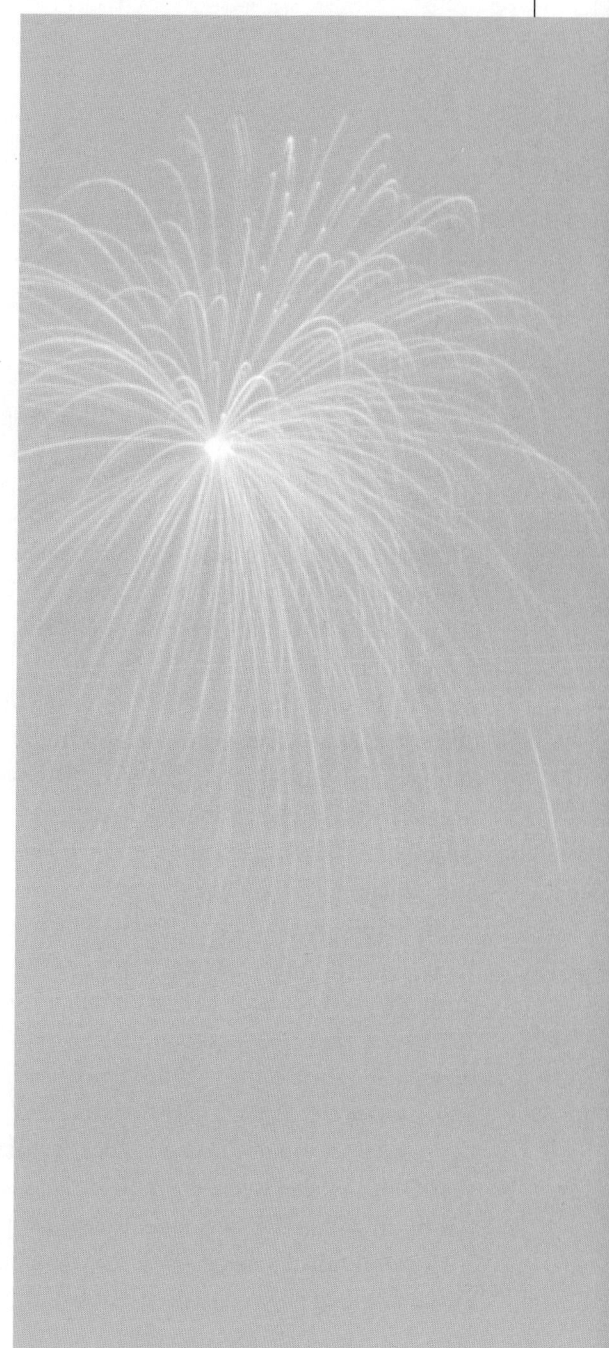

CANDLEMAS DAY FEBRUARY 2

THE GAELIC PHRASE used to describe the ancient Pagan Imbolic festival helps give a clue to the origins of this holiday: *Là fhèill Brìghde nan coinnlean* translates as "the feast day of Brìghde of the candles." "Bìghde" is Bridget of Kildare, the Celtic goddess of fire, the hearth, the blacksmith's forge, the fertile fields, poetry, and childbirth and Candlemas is the day when she visits and blesses homes.

As it did with many pagan holidays, the Christian church altered the observances attributed to Bridget of Kildare. The church made her a Christian saint and merged her observances with those used to honour the purification of the Virgin Mary and the presentation of Christ to the temple in Jerusalem. Candlemas became the day when the year's supply of church candles were blessed and a procession with lighted candles was led through the sanctuary. This symbolism marks the time when Simeon lifted the baby Jesus in his arms in the temple and proclaimed him to be the light to lighten the Gentiles.

In France, Quebec, and some Acadian communities, Candlemas is known as "la Fête de la Chandeleur." Crêpes or pancakes (often called *galettes des rois*) are eaten to insure a bountiful year. Tradition states that each member of the household must flip their own *galettes des rois*. If unsuccessful in the attempt, the participant might have bad luck for the coming year. Often a token is buried in the batter and the person finding it receives an extra measure of good luck. A special Acadian version of this ceremonial food is *crêpes à la neige* (snow crepes). Eggs were often rare at this time of winter, so people substituted them with a equal measure of hard-packed snow. The result is apparently a pancake with an amazingly light batter. Although I love to cook and bake, I haven't tried it because I live in the city and don't relish the idea of tainted "city snow" in my crêpe.

A traditional bit of folk wisdom found in Nova Scotia comes in the form of a rhyme found at Cape Sable Island and elsewhere:

Candlemas day, Candlemas day,
Half your meat and half your hay.

The rhyme means that by February 2 you should still have half the winter's provisions to see you through the remainder of the cold months. The saying goes back to mid-eighteenth-century Britain. In the *South Shore Phrase Book*, Lewis Poteet points out a connection as early as 1732 to Norfolk speech. Early settlers would have been well advised to heed such folk advice. They couldn't rush out to the supermarket to stock up on what they had overused.

Another common set of folk verses points toward the second significant celebration on this date:

If Candlemas Day be bright and fair,
You'll have two winters in one year.
If Candlemas Day be fair and bright,
Winter will take another flight.

Saint Brigid's crosses made of rushes are hung in Irish homes on Saint Brigid's Day.

GROUNDHOG DAY FEBRUARY 2

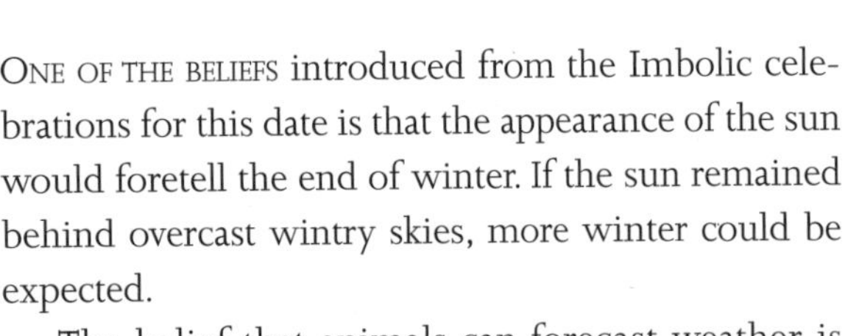

One of the beliefs introduced from the Imbolic celebrations for this date is that the appearance of the sun would foretell the end of winter. If the sun remained behind overcast wintry skies, more winter could be expected.

The belief that animals can forecast weather is ancient. It was known and practised among the Greeks and Romans. During the Middle Ages, Europeans used hibernating animals such as the bear, badger, and hedgehog to help in this divination. The merging of the two beliefs gives us a folk tradition that is today considered quaint, but is more a promotional stunt than a true folk belief. But, for years, it was a serious belief among Europeans and one they brought with them when they came to North America.

Those settlers didn't find the common European hedgehog in the New World, so they substituted similar animals—groundhogs and badgers. In Lunenburg County, German settlers introduced and observed *daks-dei* (dachs-day). *Dach* is German for "badger."

> *If a bear sees his shadow...he will go back in his den and stay six weeks longer, six more weeks of winter.* (Fauset)

Whatever the animal, it's certain he or she isn't making an appearance for the benefit of weather prognosticators. It's looking for a mate! And, in days gone by, it used to be that the forecast was predicted whenever the animal appeared. Once the custom became part of popular folklore, the media needed an accurate air time, so the convenient hour of noon was chosen for the creature to make its well-heralded entrance.

Today there are many groundhogs vying for top billing in groundhog stardom. We have Gary the Groundhog and Wiarton Willie in Ontario, and the most famous of all—Punxsutawney Phil, in Pennsylvania. Lately, Nova Scotia has been toting it own groundhog luminary. Shubenacadie Sam, who makes his home appropriately enough at the Shubenacadie Wildlife Park, is now seen on national television by millions of viewers. He didn't make any great entrance the last time I saw him being asked to give his predictions. If anything, he was blissfully unaware of his stature and had to be pushed out of his enclosure.

How correct are his forecasts? Meteorological studies show the groundhog's predictions to be only thirty per cent accurate. Not a great track record. And he certainly didn't forecast the great Groundhog Day storm of 1976, when southwestern Nova Scotia had its worst storm on record. Winds, rain, floods, and huge waves ravaged much of the Fundy shore and devastated Digby.

Shrove Tuesday is a moveable feast to mark the last day before Lent leading to Easter celebrations. Originally a day for the confession and forgiveness of sins—(a time to shrove—to pardon or purge), it is also the day when people decide to give something up, to forego a luxury as a mark of penitence. This might have been hard to do in the ancient monasteries when Shrove Tuesday was also the traditional tasting and testing day for beer and ale.

Most pre-Lenten celebrations involve using up fats and animal products from the larder and eating some kind of fried cake or bun. As the last day of Mardi Gras celebrations, Fat Tuesday marks the end of carnivals and revels. The Germans call it *fastnacht* ("fast night") or *Fasnakdei*. During his tenure, Pope Gregory the Great decreed that one must abstain from "flesh meat" and from all things that come from flesh, such as milk, cheese, eggs, and butter. The rules were occasionally stretched to the limit: in some instances, rabbit embryos cut from the womb were eaten during Lent because animals not naturally born were not considered meat.

While Elizabethans used to celebrate with dog tossing and cock fights, our traditional celebrations in Nova Scotia are considerably tamer. Lione Poirier, an Acadian historian from the Fundy shore, has documented her remembrances of young people dressing up in their best clothes for what they called Mardi Gras. This took place only on Shrove Tuesday. They visited from house to house, sang songs, including "Parton la Mer et Belle," and enjoyed homemade fudge. They played harmless tricks on each other and the festivities ended sharply at the stroke of midnight—the beginning of Lent. In many of the Acadian communities, the church bells would not be rung until Lent was over.

Another common name for Shrove Tuesday is Pancake Day. Old-world folklore says that eating pancakes on Shrove Tuesday and peas on Ash Wednesday will keep you in money for the coming year. Early Anglo Saxons offered gifts of cakes to the sun god to bring back the summer. This rite, mixed with the need to eat up fat from the larder, merged to form the tradition of eating pancakes. In fact, in Britain, a bell

called the pancake bell used to be rung from the churches to remind the women to use up the last of the fat and butter before Lent.

A quaint custom still carried on in England today is the traditional pancake race. Its origins are said to come from the time a woman, in the town of Olney, missed hearing the pancake bell and ran to the church carrying her frying pan with the pancake still in it. Whether the story is true may never be known. We do know, however, that the Olney Pancake Race has been held since 1445.

But the tradition of pancakes is not merely a British one. In almost all Christian cultures people eat some sort of baked or fried dough on this day. The Poles eat *paczki* (jelly buns), and in Nova Scotia, residents of Lunenburg County with a German background enjoy fasnak, a yeast-raised doughnut. Here, and in other parts of the province, people also make flapjacks from bread dough, which they fry on the top of the stove and serve with molasses. But whether you call them flapjacks, blintzes, crepes, waffles, griddle cakes, or just plain old pancakes, there is one bit of old folk advice you may find interesting: if you don't eat pancakes on Shrove Tuesday, you won't have any luck with your chickens.

LENT

FEBRUARY

SAXONS CALLED THIS TIME of year *lencten-monath* ("length month") because the hours of daylight were getting longer than those of darkness. The Old English word *lente* means "springtime."

Lent was eventually fixed in the eighth century B.C. at forty days—the number forty being one of many significant numbers in the Bible. It is a time of fasting and contemplation leading up to the most holy Christian celebrations of Easter. Lent begins on Ash Wednesday, the day after Shrove Tuesday.

Marry in Lent, sure to repent.

Priest in Lenten vestments.

VALENTINE'S DAY FEBRUARY 14

VALENTINE'S DAY IS BELIEVED to be the time when birds mate for life. An ancient holiday, it has become most lucrative for those selling cards, flowers, and candy. The list of valentine tokens is endless—from simple hand-made notes to elaborate paper structures I call "guilt cards"; from a single red rose to a full floral tribute; or from a heart-shaped box of chocolates to skimpy edible underwear. It's a day of chaste love and unbridled lust and its origins combine elements of both chastity and passion.

Valentine's Day and its traditions originated in two separate Roman feasts: Lupercalia and the feast day of Juno Februata.

Lupercalia was the ancient Roman festival of sexual license. By the first century B.C., even the pagan Romans didn't know its origins, but some historians suggest it might have been associated with a ceremony to protect the city and its inhabitants from wolves. The rites involved a secret band of male priests, known as Luperci, who met in the Lupercal cave on the Palantine Hill in Rome, and conducted the festival on or near February 15.

The month of February was sacred to Juno Februata, the goddess of love. (*Febris* in Latin.) She was also the goddess of women and of marriage and February 14 was her day. On that day, young men would draw the names of single women from a box. The man and woman were then paired up to form a temporary liaison, where sexual licentiousness was encouraged. The couple would hold to this bond for a period of twelve months, after which they could part company or marry.

The Christian church was opposed to this custom and offered an alternative. Instead of the names of young women, those of saints were placed in the box and the young men were expected to draw from that source and emulate the life of the saint they chose. This was obviously not always a popular alternative. By the fourteenth century the older custom was being revived and in the sixteenth century the church tried again to alter the custom. This time it was successful in eliminating the drawing of women for pair-bonding. Various pagan elements of the custom were removed and the love gods associated with the

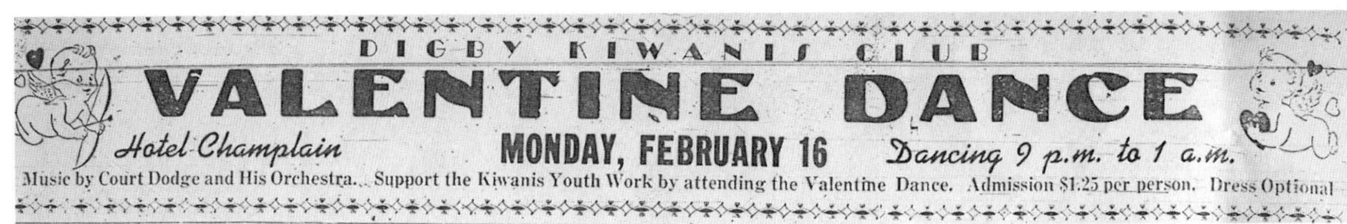

To my Valentine
If you have the trading instinct,
Answer honestly, I pray,
Will you swap your Bachelor's Button
For my bleeding heart to-day?
?
!

Valentine card c.1925, from the C.E. Bell collection, Dartmouth Heritage Museum.

celebration were replaced with a far more tame representation of love—St. Valentine.

Historians can't agree on the real story of St. Valentine. Many origins are connected to his pedigree. The one most allied to church tradition says St. Valentine was a young bishop living and practising his faith near Rome around 270 A.D.. This was about the time when Roman emperor Claudius II issued an edict forbidding marriage to insure more single men for his armies. Valentine disagreed and, wanting to give young lovers a Christian marriage, performed the ceremony in secret. Claudius had the bishop arrested and imprisoned, although the emperor was impressed with the piety and devotion of the young priest and made attempts to have Valentine denounce Christianity and recognize the Roman gods. When Valentine refused, he was scheduled for execution.

While he languished in prison awaiting his fate, Valentine met the blind daughter of his jailer, Apterous. Apterous asked him to heal his daughter and, according to legend, through pure Christian love and faith, her sight was restored. Just before his execution, Valentine asked for a pen and paper from his jailer, and sent her a farewell message, signing it "from your Valentine." The traditional date of his death is February 14.

In these types of stories, the line between fact and legend is often blurred. But, when the church merged the ancient pagan rites of Lupercalia and Februata with the story of Valentine's chaste love for the spiritual well-being of the jailer's blind daughter, the legend grew and ensconced the martyred bishop as the patron saint of lovers. Other legends concerning St. Valentine came later. The crocus, which often flowers around February 14, is called St. Valentine's flower.

The little naked cherub with the bow and quiver of arrows is another of the Valentine symbols. In ancient Greece the cherub was known as Eros, the young son of Aphrodite, the goddess of love and beauty. To the Romans, he was Cupid, and his mother was Venus. He was responsible for impregnating a number of goddesses and mortals—certainly more symbolic than shooting a love arrow into a sweetheart's heart. The symbol of the lover's pure (yet pierced) heart has become the most common icon on Valentine letters and cards everywhere.

Out of the custom of retrieving names of young women from a box has evolved a day when large sums of money are spent on love messages, and the manufacturing and promotion of Valentine cards has become a huge industry. But, it took several centuries for the idea of spiritual love to be dropped altogether, and personal love messages to become the norm. The messages, as well as the persons receiving them, became known as valentines. *Poor Robin's Almanac* of 1683 reminded maidens to choose a Valentine in "this the leaping month." However, by 1830, the *Catholic Annals* complained: "The vulgar custom of sending Valentines on this day had its origin in an endeavor of several zealous persons of the clerical order to put an end to the superstitious practice of boys drawing by lots the names of girls…Instead of this custom they permitted the names of saints to be drawn. These got the names of Valentines, but being afterwards much

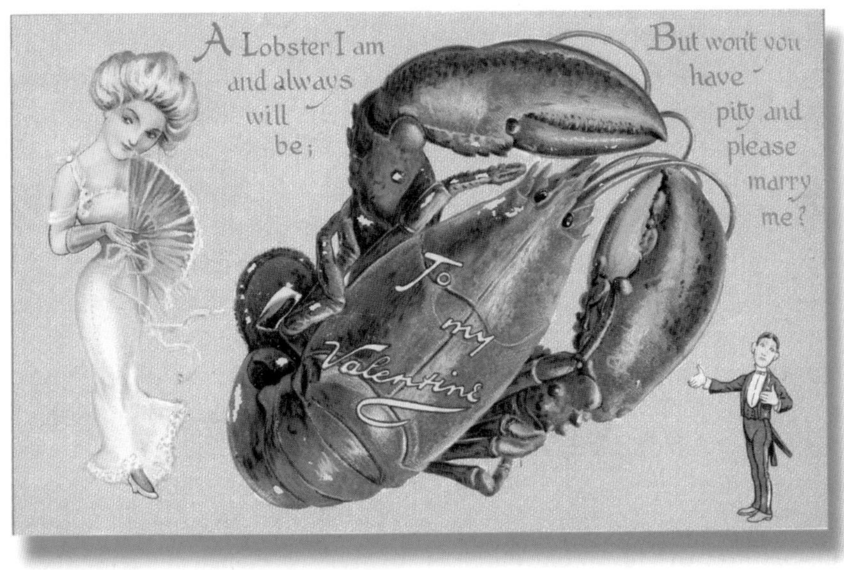
A Lobster I am
and always
will
be;
But won't you
have
pity and
please
marry
me?
To my Valentine

A valentine inscribed to Master Harry Starr, Port Williams, 1914.

abused and converted into love letters, the ceremony degenerated again into a pagan and foolish custom."

One of the earliest Valentine's Day cards on record was sent in 1415 by Charles, Duke of Orleans, to his wife while he was a prisoner in the Tower of London. The card is now preserved in the British Museum.

The earliest advertisement I could find in the Nova Scotian newspapers comes from the *Nova Scotian* for February 6, 1840. It was one simple cutline: "Valentine Letter Writers; valentine letters, Valentine Envelopes, etc. C. H. Belcher." Twenty-seven years later, several issues of the *British Colonist*, for February 1867, announced that valentines could be purchased in Halifax at William Gossip's and Z.S. Hall's.

Although the newspaper ads didn't carry illustrations of these valentines, we know from collections of vintage cards that they were elaborate, pressed-paper cards, printed in colour, many of which are now considered valuable antiques by collectors. For those who couldn't, or didn't, choose to send store-bought cards, a hand-made card was treasured for its personal touch. When the late nineteenth-century mail order and seed catalogues became available to the masses, these colourful and free publications became popular sources for pretty pictures and posies used to decorate cards. Tinsel from cigarette and tea packages, lace, crepe paper and coloured tissue paper all made their way to the pages of the love tokens.

Joke cards were very popular in the latter part of the nineteenth century. Boys called them "comics" and "prettys." They were delivered on the evening of February 13 and were announced by the blowing of tin horns and rattles before the jokester took flight to watch from a distance. One of the most popular games was to chalk a square on the front step to resemble an envelope and then watch the receiver try to pick it up. Of course, this would only be done by naughty children—never any of the members of the popular Rainbow Club, featured in the *Halifax Herald* in the 1920s and 1930s. The congenial Farmer Brown, who oversaw the club's activities, was quick to remind the kiddies, "It is fun to have a valentine box in school and send valentines to one's school mates—nice ones of course. No Rainbow would think of sending any other kind!"

I fondly remember the valentine's boxes we had in our classrooms in Halifax and Sherbrooke. Usually made by the teacher, or by one of the more creative children, the boxes were covered with white tissue paper and decorated with hearts and other valentine symbols. Some of the children made their own cards but for the most part we used Valentines bought in books or loose packets. There was always one for the teacher, for parents, and a few special ones to be given to your very best "secret" love.

Although through the years the popular images have changed, the messages remain the same: "Will you be mine? Be My Love! Be My Valentine!" Where once these invocations were printed on cards bearing the images of everything from Mickey Mouse to the Beatles, they are now found on cards featuring the likenesses of one of the many popular "boy bands" or

Harry Potter. But, as they say, it's the thought that counts. Today, you can even send your true love an e-valentine. Just choose the card you want on the internet, add your message, point and click, and off it flies as Cupid's arrow did of yore. But, call me old-fashioned, cyber-valentines just don't cut it. You get the job done, but you don't get to see the look in her eyes when she reads your message!

Other Valentine trends come and go. Valentine teas were a popular tradition in Nova Scotia during the 1920s. One of the most prestigious was the Ashburn Tea, held at the golf club of that name in Halifax. It was a social highlight of the season. It's now more common to find churches holding Valentines teas and socials.

Gifts of chocolates or other sweets have been replaced with health-conscious offerings of gift certificates for facials or concert tickets. But, if your pockets are empty, there's one gift that cost nothing yet is the most valuable—just say I love you. (Unless you want to take a page from the book of a swain on Nova Scotia's eastern shore, who thought so much of his true love that he sent her the best gift he could think of—a bucket of salt herring!)

The first person you see of the opposite sex on Valentine's Day will be your valentine.

Twist the stem of an apple and say the letters of the alphabet. The stem will break off at the initial of your true love.

Peel an apple, making the peelings as long and intact as you can. Throw them over your shoulder and they will land forming the initial of your true love.

Eat salt fish; go to bed; your future lover will bring you a glass of water.

NATIONAL FLAG DAY OF CANADA FEBRUARY 15

NATIONAL FLAG DAY has only been an official holiday in Canada since 1996, when Prime Minister Jean Chrétien set February 15 aside to honour our flag.

The bold, red maple leaf on a background of red and white is recognized around the world. In fact, travellers from other countries sometimes sew a Canadian flag to their backpack or jacket because it's the symbol that opens doors and ensures a polite response. Safe to say, its one of the most respected icons in the world.

It didn't always have such a smooth ride. Even today, many older Canadians remember the previous flag, the Red Ensign, with fondness. When, at the stroke of noon on February 15, 1965, Canada's present flag was raised for the very first time, some called it "Pearson's Rag," a derogatory remark aimed at the prime minister of the day, Lester B. Pearson. It was under his leadership that Canada adopted its new national symbol. Today, there's a whole generation of Canadians who have grown up knowing no other flag.

Of all the provinces, it is Nova Scotia that stands unique in Canada's flag history as the only province in Canada, and the first colony of Great Britain, to have been granted, by royal charter, a flag of its own. This came about long before Nova Scotia was a province of Canada.

In 1621, James I of Scotland granted Sir William Alexander "all lands lying between New England and Newfoundland." Later, to raise money for the colonization of these lands, King Charles I of England recognized James' proclamation and created the title of

Canada Day Program celebrating 25 years of the new flag.

baronet. In 1625 the new baronets were granted the right to bear the new coat of arms on their personal armorial shields.

While the original record describing the arms (the armorial or heraldic shield) has been lost, we know its design from the early nineteenth-century registry of His Majesty's Lyon Office at Edinburgh, where a description was re-entered. It bore the cross of Saint Andrew (blue on a white ground), charged with an escutcheon of the royal arms of Scotland (a lion on a shield). The arms had iconoclastic symbols known as supporters: a unicorn and what was then commonly called, a "savage," representing the new world: an image of so-called "primitive people" representing the subjugation of the local inhabitants to the new order. In most contemporary flags such symbols has been adapted to represent the First Nations of the region.

An examination of Nova Scotia's flag today shows a more simple design than the one described in the nineteenth century. For the most part the arms were used on documents and shields, rather than on an actual flag. In 1858 a flag resembling our present one was flown at Halifax's Natal Day celebrations. It was designed by Dr. Cogswell, who also designed the kingfisher emblem for the city.

After Confederation, the College of Heralds was asked to provide coats of arms for the four original provinces. Unaware that Nova Scotia already had an arms, they devised a new one featuring a salmon and three thistles. Although some moved to have this new arms dismissed, most Nova Scotians didn't know about it. It wasn't until 1929 that the authorities were asked to revoke the newest arms in favour of the original one. The use of the first arms, as granted in 1625, without the supporters and crest, was authorized by royal warrant as the official flag of Nova Scotia on January 19, 1929.

Arms of Nova Scotia—the original at left and one designed by the College of Heralds after Confederation.

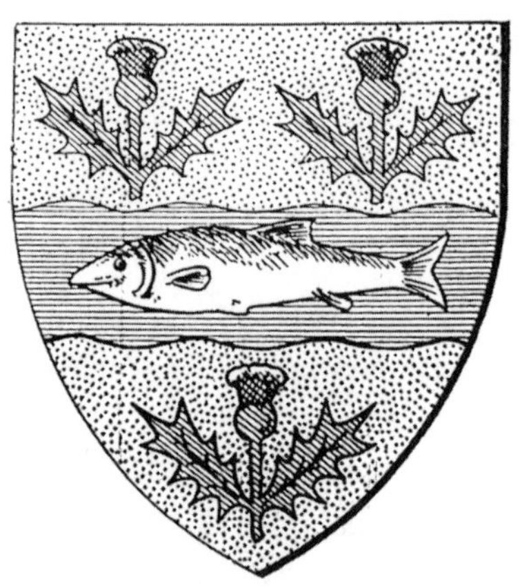

MARCH

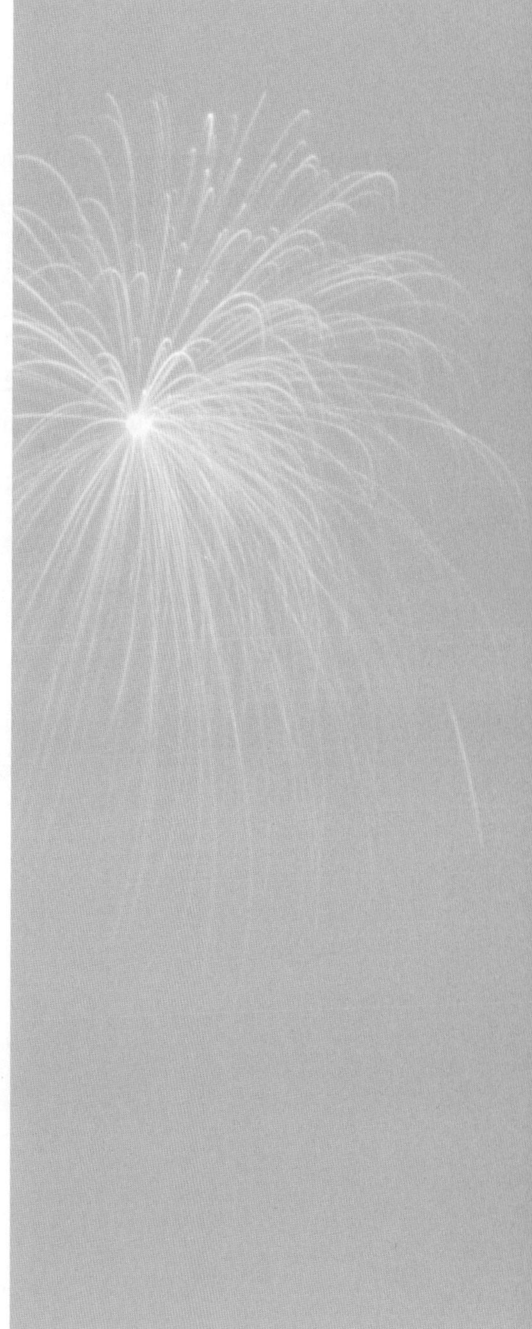

ST. DAVID'S DAY

MARCH 1

St. David is the patron saint of Wales. He was born around the middle of the fifth century in Wales and was reputed to be a relative of King Arthur. As a young man he entered a monastery on the Isle of Wight and prepared himself for a life of missionary work among the Britons. According to legend, he led his countrymen against the Saxons and had his army wear leeks in their hats to distinguish them from their foes. Another legend in Wales tells of daffodils springing from the earth on the first day of March in his honour.

Although Nova Scotia doesn't have a large population of people of Welsh heritage, a daffodil in a lapel or a leek in a hatband can still be seen here and there on March 1 to honour St. David.

Gan feddwl amdanoch
ar Ddydd Gwl Dewi Sant

ST. PATRICK'S DAY MARCH 17

St. Patrick was born in the later half of the fourth century A.D. Some historians claim he was born in England; other legends claim France or Wales as his motherland. Much of what we know about his life comes from a book he is supposed to have written near the end of his life titled *The Confession*. It begins: "I am Patrick, a sinner, most uncultivated and least of all the faithful."

At the age of sixteen, when he claimed he "did not then know the true God," he was carried off by a band of Irish marauders. Irish tradition says he tended the herds of a chieftain in County Antrim, where he was kept in bondage for six years. Patrick's mission in Ireland lasted for over twenty years. He died on March 17, 461 A.D., and that day has been commemorated in his honour ever since.

After St. Patrick's death, various stories of his great works and miracles grew, so by the end of the seventh century, he had become a legendary figure. It was said that the shamrock, an ancient symbol for the triple goddess Bridget, was used by Patrick to explain the concept of the Christian trinity. Legend also tells how he put the curse of God on venomous snakes in Ireland and drove them all into the sea where they were drowned.

Other symbols of Irish culture, not necessarily associated directly with St. Patrick, have become important icons in the celebration of his day. The

St Patrick's Day Parade, Halifax, twentieth century.

Celtic harp is an ancient instrument used to accompany poets and storytellers. The leprechaun, the mischievous elf of Celtic lore, has become one of the holiday's most enduring symbols.

While St. Patrick's Day is certainly celebrated with gusto in Ireland, it is an even more popular holiday in North America. Where it once honoured Irish heritage and the life of a saint, it has become a time for parties, Irish music, and a lot of drinking. Folks of any nationality and ethnicity can be seen sporting t-shirts and buttons reading "Kiss Me, I'm Irish!" Parades, green beer, plastic hats, shamrocks, the "wearing o' the green," and an Irish feast are all popular customs in Canada and the United States. Even the typical "Irish" dinner of corned beef and cabbage is more a derivation of the boiled dinner popular with the early settlers on this side of the pond.

It was those early Irish settlers to Nova Scotia that overcame the class system that made being Irish something to be scorned. At one time an area in Halifax was known (derogatorily) as Irish Town. But Irish immigrants worked hard to overcome the many biases held against them. For years they walked an odd line between being accepted in social circles and having few political and religious rights. Still, because of determination and keen social and political alliances, they succeeded in becoming major players in the development of the colony.

The Charitable Irish Society was founded in Halifax in 1786. That same year, their first St. Patrick's Day feast included such guests as His Royal Highness Prince Edward, Sir John Wentworth, certain members of the Privy Council, and members of the House of Assembly. The society provided for widows and orphans of deceased subscribers, and went on to make great progress in establishing people of Irish heritage as equal citizens in the province.

My maternal ancestors left Ireland in the eighteenth century to come to Nova Scotia. Their legacy to me is a proud heritage of working-class people who loved music and knew how to have a great party!

MI-CARÊME

MI-CARÊME (middle of Lent) originated in France in the Middle Ages and was traditionally held on the third Thursday of the forty days of Lent. It was an opportunity to allow people to escape their Lenten duties for a brief respite of fun and indulgences. The celebration was brought to New France but seems to have survived in Canada in only a handful of communities in Quebec, on the Magdelan Islands, and in the regions of Chéticamp, St-Joseph-du-Moine, and Margaree in Cape Breton.

The tradition is similar to mumming, where participants dress in disguises, visit homes in the community, and sometimes receive treats. Traditional elements vary from district to district. Along the Fundy coast on Nova Scotia's French Shore children enjoyed the Mi-Carême traditions of wearing costumes and masks, but received no treats.

Mi-Carême was originally held for one day only but now has grown to a multi-day celebration. In Cape Breton, it was broken up into two categories. Mi-Carême Eve was called La Petite Mi-Carême and was reserved for the children. Like the children along the French Shore, Cape Breton youth would disguise themselves and go from house to house. But, in Cape Breton, the children broke their Lenten fast by accepting treats for this one day only.

The following day was the adults' turn. At the turn of the twentieth century, celebrations at L'Ardoise, in Cape Breton, lasted for several days. In the early years, the folks going door to door were exclusively young men. The revellers, called Mi-Carêmes, announced their arrival by ringing bells and banging cudgels on the door. Once admitted to the house, they would be offered a drink followed by dancing to the music of fiddles and accordions. Throughout all the festivities, the Mi-Carêmes tried to hide their identity under their costumes and masks and by disguising their voices.

A folk character is also associated with the celebration. Her name—La Mi-Carême! Tradition says she wanders about the village dressed in a long robe with a hood, leaving gifts for the children on La Petite Mi-Carême in stockings or hats left out to receive the goodies.

At Chezzetcook, the women of the village dressed up in white sheets with eye holes cut out. They came around to the schoolyard at recess and brought treats of sugar cookies, gingersnaps, and small cakes. The children would chase them calling out, "Mi-Carême, Donnez moi un gâteau." The treats were tossed and scrambled, then the women would dash off again to be chased through the fields by the children. Once she had tossed away all her treats, the woman representing La Mi-Carême chased the children away with a cane or long fork.

La Mi-Carême was not always seen as a benevolent character—she could punish children if they didn't obey their parents. Children who were not asleep after seven o'clock were told to watch out for her. The same Mi-Carême is also said to be the one responsible for transporting babies from heaven to their new earthly homes.

La Mi-Carême's image is a popular one for Mi-Carême costumes and masks. These guises were traditionally made at home with whatever was at hand. Old clothes were turned inside out, or cut up and remade. Masks could be simple cloth sacks drawn over the wearer's head with a face applied with left-over paints.

In the past few years, some celebrants have taken to renting costumes from local business who specialize in Mi-Carême disguises. It is not uncommon to see some people change costumes several times a day to avoid detection. Today's costumes can range from those seen at Halloween to those that reflect Acadian cultural figures such as la Sagouine and Évangeline. One of the most popular images in the Chéticamp area is a figure called Le Moine (The Friar), named for a rock that was a landmark for the local fishermen until it fell into the sea.

Le Moine and many other figures are being represented in new masks being made by Acadie Masques, a non-profit organization in Cape Breton formed with help from Fédération Acadienne de la Nouvelle-Écosse and corporate sponsorship to promote Acadian culture and arts. Mi-Carême mask makers using traditional and contemporary techniques have set up studios in St Joseph-du-Moine.

It is fascinating to see traditional folk art and the cultural celebrations connected with it being morphed with twenty-first-century technologies. Where the Mi-Carême activities used to be confined to walking distance in a village, today, with the automobile, participants can travel to any district they like. In recent years, this has meant many more participants at each home—in some cases, two to three hundred Mi-Carêmes in one night. Many people now receive Mi-Carêmes in their garages, while in other places the community hall is used. Decorations are erected and signs are posted to announce a spot where Mi-Carêmes are welcome. A tourist event that draws visitors from all over the province and abroad, Mi-Carême has become so popular that the original holiday has been stretched to last seven days. A web site has even been developed to further the preservation of the Mi-Carême tradition (http://collections.ic.gc.ca/micareme/). This is how a traditional custom, once isolated to a few communities and celebrated by a handful of people has, thanks to modern influences, been revised and altered to suit contemporary society, proving that folk tradition is alive and evolving.

EASTER

THE VARIOUS EASTER CELEBRATIONS are calculated from the date on which Easter Sunday falls, which is the first Sunday after the first full moon after spring equinox. The name of the celebration is derived from Eostre, the Anglo-Saxon goddess of spring. A festival in her honour was celebrated at the vernal equinox.

Easter is the most important festival of Christianity. It celebrates the resurrection of Jesus Christ on the third day after he was crucified—the foundation on which Christianity is based. But, like most Christian holidays, the secular customs associated with Easter draw aspects of their beliefs and rites from pagan and non-Christian sources. Rabbits, eggs, and bonnets are all part of the Easter iconography, but it is the events surrounding the final days of Jesus Christ on earth that are significant to Christianity. Each day of Holy Week has particular significance:

Palm Sunday—the Sunday preceding Easter Sunday recalls Christ's triumphant entry into Jerusalem one week before his crucifixion.

Holy Monday—commemorates Christ's cleansing the temple of money lenders.

Holy Tuesday—recalls Christ's description to his disciples on the Mount of Olives of the destruction of Jerusalem.

Holy Wednesday—once called Spy Wednesday, recalls Judas's decision to betray Christ.

Maundy Thursday—commemorates Christ's Last Supper with his disciples, his agony in the Garden of Gethsemane, and his arrest. From the Latin mandatum ("entrust" or "enjoin"), Maundy has held the long-standing tradition that people in authority in the Church wash the feet of those serving under them.

Good Friday—recalls Christ's crucifixion.

Holy Saturday—Easter Eve, the final day of Holy Week and of Lent.

Easter Sunday—commemorates Christ's resurrection.

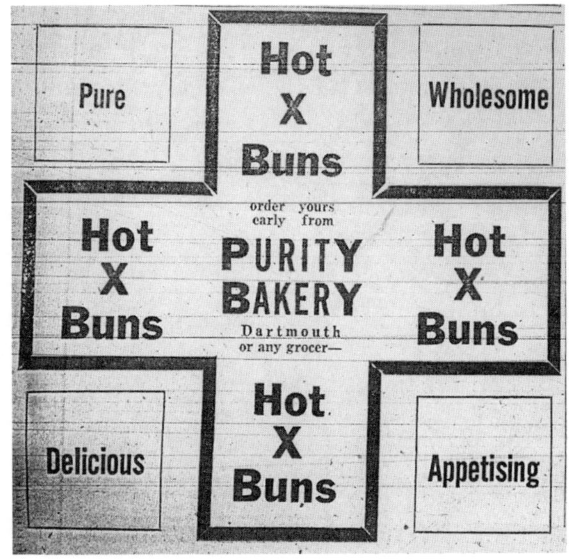

The two most important days of Holy Week are Good Friday and Easter Sunday. Aside from the rituals of the Christian church, many folk beliefs are associated with these two days. And in many examples, the beliefs of the church and the secular rites blur—take, for example, hot cross buns.

These buns are traditionally baked on Good Friday using yeast dough formed into rounds, sometimes with the addition of raisins, and topped with slits or icing in the shape of an X or a cross. During the feast to honour Eostre, an ox was sacrificed and its horns were displayed for the duration of the springtime celebrations. Symbolic horns in the form of a symmetrical cross were used to decorate the ritual bread made for the occasion. Some etymologists believe our present word "bun" is derived from the Saxon word "boun" which means "sacred ox." Its an easy move from these Saxon buns to the ones decorated with the Christian symbol of the cross.

An interesting belief associated with hot cross buns was that they last throughout the year. In many homes, one bun would be set aside for the year to protect the house from fire and flood, and sailors would take one to sea to protect them from disease and shipwreck.

Another belief recorded by Helen Creighton at Whynacht's Settlement in Nova Scotia is that it was the custom on Good Friday to pick teaberry (wintergreen) leaves for making tea.

Bake bread on Good Friday and take a bun and put it away. It will never spoil or mould, but will dry up and get hard. The ship you carry it in or the house you live in will never sink or burn. (Creighton)

If a witch bothers you, take certain words from the Bible, go to the door on Good Friday at sunrise and make a wish. Whoever is the witch will come at daylight and die at your door. To keep witches from your house, make crosses out of dogwood and new pins to put above each door and window before Easter morning. (Creighton)

Never take the cattle out of the barn on Good Friday—it's bad luck. (Creighton)

If the sun shines on Good Friday you will have a hot dry summer. (Creighton)

To ensure a good crop, sow cabbage seeds on Good Friday. (Creighton)

Easter Sunday is acknowledged as the most important celebration for Christians because it commemorates the resurrection of Christ. In many Christian communities it is marked by a service at sunrise. An earlier, yet similar, custom can be traced to the ancient pagan custom of holding a ceremony at dawn to welcome the sun at the vernal equinox. This was a celebration of spring, which the ancient peoples considered a rebirth or resurrection of the natural elements.

In many Christian denominations, Easter is a special time for baptisms. It was an especially important part of the Easter sunrise service at the Seaview United Baptist Church at Africville, once an African-Canadian community in Halifax. Church members and their guests, who came from all over the province, gathered to participate in ceremonies at what was known as "The Singing Church." The service would begin at 5:00 A.M. and continue until noon. Then the congregation would walk down the road to the shores of the Bedford Basin, where new initiates would be baptised in the cold waters of Halifax Harbour.

In 1967, Dr. Helen Creighton secured funding from the Canadian Folk Music Society to record African Nova Scotian music. She contracted Marvin Burke to record what was to become the last Easter sunrise service at the Seaview United Baptist Church. Later that year the church was bulldozed and its community uprooted in one of Canada's most shameful acts of urban resettlement.

On Easter morning, if there is snow on the ground and you melted it, it was a cure for cattle. (Creighton)

The sun dances on Easter morning. Look through a piece of black silk. Some say the sun dances on Easter morning. (Creighton)

Crows flying over the house on Easter means death. (Fauset)

Collect dogwood before sunrise Easter Sunday to make a cross to place over the door or on the door sill. (Creighton)

In Nova Scotia there are many secular customs and beliefs surrounding the Easter season. In Shelburne County, children erected Easter camps in the woods. On Good Friday they would build shelters out of brush and evergreen boughs. The boys' camps were deep in the woods, while those made by girls were closer to home. Sometimes boys and girls worked together to build a camp at a mutually agreed upon spot. On Cape Sable Island, children aged four to fifteen headed off to their camps at 7:00 A.M. on Easter Monday. An important part of the custom was the picnic lunch they took with them. No simple affair, it could include hard boiled eggs, homemade bread and molasses, and, sometimes, lobster.

From the latter part of the nineteenth century and up to the 1950s it was traditional to wear new clothes to church on Easter Sunday and, for women, a new hat. Easter bonnets hark back to adornment associated with ancient fertility rites when maidens wore wreaths of spring flowers in their hair to greet the gods of the new year.

The origin of the Easter gift basket, used to collect eggs and receive gifts, can be traced, in part, to medieval times. Baskets filled with food prepared for the Easter feast were taken to church to be blessed on Easter morning. During the fourth century, eating eggs during Lent was banned. But, since spring is a productive time for egg-laying hens, people began to cook the eggs in their shells to preserve them. These eggs were often taken to church in the Easter baskets to be blessed along with the rest of the food.

Eggs were not only used as food, but also as symbols of older, pre-Christian beliefs. The Latin proverb, *Omne vivum ex ovo* ("All life comes from an egg"), is a nod to the ancient belief held by many people around the world that the universe was created out of an egg. Therefore, its not surprising to find the egg is a symbol of life.

Pre-Christian Europeans would hang this life-symbol on trees in midsummer. Eggs were believed to have regenerative powers and to contain a life force. When used as ceremonial talismans, they were considered sacred. Christianity adopted and added to many of the beliefs surrounding the power of eggs. It was believed that if you kept an egg laid on Good Friday for a hundred years, its yolk would turn into a diamond. Similarly, Good Friday eggs cooked on Easter Sunday were said to promote the fertility of the trees and crops and protect against sudden deaths.

Since eggs were said to have magical powers, it is only natural for people to try to bring some of that magic their way. One of the most common ways to appropriate power is through consumption. Therefore, if a large number of eggs are eaten, the power received will be proportional. Easter morning egg-eating contests were once popular in Nova Scotia. That is, before we learned what we know about cholesterol and its effects.

Another common pastime now gone out of fashion is egg tipping. People throughout the province used to gather eggs and hold a contest to see who had the strongest egg. Two opponents would each hold an egg in their hand and rap them against each other. Many believed brown eggs to be stronger than white eggs. The game was won by the person whose egg remained intact. I've heard stories of people cheating by using hard boiled eggs or by filling emptied-out shells with wax. Strengthening an egg by soaking it in vinegar could make it last longer but gave a softer shell. The victor was awarded the title of "king tipper," which was also the name given to the winning egg!

Dyeing eggs was, and still is, a popular Easter custom. Some people speculate the eggs were dyed to trick the evil forces into not recognizing them as real eggs. Other suggest it was a way to "gild the lily," making a precious token even more alluring and pleasing to the gods. In ancient times eggs were dyed and eaten at spring festivals in Egypt, Persia, Greece, and Rome. The art and tradition of dying eggs was most likely introduced into European custom by returning Crusaders. When artisans began adding symbols to the coloured eggs, they became small works of art. One need only look at a beautiful Ukrainian Easter egg to appreciate the complex and intricate designs and symbols.

Traditional egg dyeing in Nova Scotia probably began with natural dyes such as onion skin yellow, madder red, and stains made from lamp black. By the nineteenth century, special dye papers were available but those without the means to buy them used non-colourfast tissue papers. Today children can get egg-dyeing kits, complete with instructions and decals of Easter motifs. These painted and dyed eggs are most often saved for display and decoration, while candy eggs are used for egg hunts.

Hunting for Easter eggs is still a popular pastime for young and old alike. Acadian children along the Fundy shore went out after church on Easter Sunday and searched for coloured eggs in moss-covered baskets. In Sonora the children hunted for eggs nestled between rocks or under trees in what my father remembers as "bunny nests." At Riverport, nests were filled with coloured eggs, while at Blandford children set out their caps, lined with spruce boughs, for the Easter bunny to fill. It was quite common for children in Nova Scotia to put out a hat or cap to receive treats delivered by the Easter bunny on Easter Sunday morning. I did it 'til I was a big boy—and would probably do it still if I thought I would get anything!

But, why does a bunny deliver Easter eggs and other treats? To find the answer, we must go back to the beliefs surrounding the goddess Eostre. Legend tells how the hare was actually a bird until Eostre transformed it. In gratitude, the hare vowed to lay eggs for the goddess. Add that story to the fact that hares can be prolific and are a well-known symbol of fertility, and you have a significant icon of spring's rebirth and abundance. The first extant reference to the Easter hare and its eggs was published in Germany in 1572. Even today, many German children hold the Easter hare as important as Saint Nicholas.

There are many Nova Scotian beliefs surrounding hares' nests in Lunenburg County and parts of Guysborough County (where some of my relatives of German extraction come from), so the idea of searching for eggs in hares' nests makes sense. Besides, rabbits are born blind and underground; hares are born in nests above ground. And the term bunny? Some suggest it comes from the diminutive "bun," the Scottish word for hare's tail.

Easter's secular customs will continue to evolve and change. Where children once received skipping ropes, cap guns, colouring books, and egg-shaped candy or milk chocolate eggs and bunnies made especially for Easter, they can now look forward to computer games, and sour balls.

Nova Scotian riddle from Oakland: A little white house all filled with meat, no windows or doors to get in to eat. Answer: An egg. (Creighton)

Eggs without yolks are known as witch eggs. If a hen lays such an egg, she must be a witch's familiar. You must take the hen and bury her alive to destroy the familiar. (Creighton)

Take the first egg laid by a hen on Good Friday, and hide it on your person at church on Easter Sunday. You will be able to identify all the witches at church because they will have milk stools on their heads. But, they must not get near you; they know you have the egg and will try and break it, giving them power over you. (Creighton)

APRIL

APRIL FOOL'S DAY

APRIL 1

In 1995 all the buzz in Halifax was about the upcoming summer's G-7 Summit. Leaders from seven of the most economically powerful nations in the world would be meeting in Nova Scotia's capital. Preparing the city for the massive security needed for the heads of state was an ongoing topic of conversation among the citizens. The whole downtown core would be a secure zone—open only to those with passes. Barriers would be erected; bomb squads would be combing the waterfront; divers would be searching the harbour for possible sabotage. The city was being transformed. Thousands of trees were planted and repairs were made to existing structures—If it didn't move, it got painted.

Haligonians watched, amused, bewildered, and excited to be part of an event that would be putting us on the world stage. We didn't always agree with what was being erected, demolished, or changed to suit the needs of the planners, but, for the most part, we took it in stride. That is until they did the unthinkable.

The first I heard of it was on the six o'clock newscast from Halifax's ATV (Atlantic Television) supper-hour show. The news journalist's voice-over informed us that because the security people needed a clear view from Citadel Hill to the harbour, the top section of the historic town clock was being removed. The video footage showed a crane lifting the section containing the clock face off its main structure. I gasped! This time they had gone too far.

The next day, I decided to drive by and see if it was a bad as I thought. As I got near the clock it was obvious that it was still intact—unchanged since the Duke of Kent had it erected in 1803. And then, it dawned on me. Great computer graphics had fooled me!

I should have tweaked to the ruse. The day before was the first day of April. I had even played a trick on my wife earlier that morning. But, I had fallen for a classic—one of the best April Fool's Day jokes ever!

The origin of this holiday is uncertain. The concept of holding a special day to celebrate fools and for playing tricks on the unsuspecting is ancient. The Hindu festival of Holi, which falls on or close to the Gregorian calendar date of March 31, is a time when people play practical jokes and send others on false errands. Early Romans consecrated a day in honour of fools. Some people believe the Catholic church took this festival and turned it into Auld Fool's Day, which was held on the first day of January. Its move to the first of April was brought about when the end of the calendar year changed from March 31 to December 31.

In Scotland, April Fool's Day lasts forty-eight hours. The second "day" is called Taily Day and pranks involving the posterior, such as pinning on a tail or a sign, are played. The unwitting victim is called a "gowk" (an extinct cuckoo), and carrying out the joke is called "hunting the gowk"—which is why we say people are cuckoo if we want to imply they are crazy or stupid. In France, that poor sot is a *poisson d'Avril* (fish of April).

Apparently, fish newly hatched in spring are easily caught! A similar prank used to be played in Nova Scotia: paper tails and notes were surreptitiously attached to the back of school children's clothes.

While it's one thing to play a joke on an individual, the best April Fool's Day pranks are those played on many—as was the case with Halifax and the town clock. Perhaps the earliest hoax to dupe the general public took place at London on April 1, 1698. The following day a newspaper of that great city, which boasted an intelligent citizenry, was able to note: "Yesterday being the first of April several persons were sent to the Tower of London to watch the annual lion-washing ceremony." There were, indeed, lions at the Tower of London—but there was no such ceremony. Still, years later in 1856, the old trick obviously forgotten, some people actually bought tickets to the ceremony, even though the lions had been removed to the London Zoo twenty-one years before.

Although I shouldn't talk, it seems Britons were slow to learn about April Fool's Day hoaxes. But, if you can't trust the press—who can you trust? They wouldn't be allowed to print or broadcast it if it wasn't true, would they?

In 1957, the respected BBC television show *Panorama* reported on the annual spaghetti harvest in Italy. The news footage showed groups of women picking strands of spaghetti from trees and laying them in the sun to dry. Most viewers saw through the story, but some did call asking for details so they could attend the harvest the next year.

In April 1844, the *New York Sun* carried news of the first trans-Atlantic crossing by a hot air balloon. The article was filled with technical detail, including scientific reports from leading balloonists of the day. Readers were fascinated and welcomed a new age of trans-Atlantic travel. The only glitch—it was a hoax, planted by the American writer Edgar Allan Poe.

Orson Wells caused a similar stir on April 1, 1938, with his radio broadcast of H. G. Wells's tale of invading Martians. Only this time, the joke went too far. People who tuned in after the opening announcement that the broadcast of *War of the Worlds* was a work of fiction panicked. They actually thought they were in a life-and-death struggle with extraterrestrial invaders.

So, its best to keep your pranks simple. After all, the joke you play this year may come back to haunt you the next. And remember—according to popular tradition, any prank you pull must be completed by noon or else you become the fool!

The first of April, some do say,
Is set apart for All Fools' Day.
But why the people call it so,
Nor I, nor they themselves do know.
But on this day are people sent
On purpose for pure merriment.

Poor Robin's Almanac (1790)

ARBOUR DAY / EARTH DAY APRIL 22

Here is an interesting example of a once-popular North American holiday from the nineteenth and early twentieth centuries being transformed into a global celebration of a second millennium issue.

The idea for a holiday to celebrate nature, and especially the planting of trees, originally came from J. Sterling Morton, in Nebraska, later the United States' secretary of agriculture. Morton had a passion to replant the forests which had been obliterated by settlers moving west. His idea was to get the youth of the nation involved and he proposed a program where school children would gather on a spring day and plant trees. He called it Arbour Day.

Arbour Day was first introduced in Canada from the United States in the 1880s. It was perhaps first celebrated in Nova Scotia in 1885, when William Ackhurst, chairman for the Halifax City School Commission, advised government authorities in his annual report: "I am glad to be able to report the complete success which attended our first Arbour Day. Pupils, teachers and citizens all contributed their part." After describing the formal addresses and remarks by officials, he added: "A large number of ornamental trees were set out, which will eventually add much to the appearance of the city....In many cases the interest elicited led to the planting of trees around the homes of the pupils. I would recommend that an Arbour Day be set apart for the whole province."

Although it seems Arbour Day was never made an official Canadian holiday, it remained popular with school children well into the 1940s. Often led by Boy Scout troops, it was an opportunity for students to escape the classroom for a day and get outdoors. Many teachers and civic leaders saw it as an opportunity to instill local community pride. In Shelburne County it was a time for the girls to clean the school from top to bottom, while the boys worked on the grounds, clearing brush and planting. Work was completed by noon followed by a picnic and games, especially baseball.

Arbour Day had all but disappeared from school activities in Canada by the late 1950s. Then, the 1960s brought back youth awareness to environmental issues and, once again, a special day was set aside to recognize the need to look after the planet. First launched in the United States as an environmental awareness event in 1970, organizers of Earth Day took the date of Arbour Day, a logical tie-in with the former holiday and acknowledged by many as the birth of the modern environmental movement. Canadian environmentalists joined soon after and, for a number of years, it was a grassroots celebration said to be celebrated by hippies and so-called "tree huggers." But, by 1990, Canadians joined with two hundred million people in 141 nations around the world to celebrate the first International Earth Day. Statistics gathered by Earth Day supporters show that by the year 2000 more than six million Canadians, including nearly every school child in Canada, was participating in an Earth Day activity. Although the day has now moved far beyond the planting of trees, it is good to see that William Ackhurst's recommendations from 1885 are still being validated.

ST. GEORGE'S DAY

APRIL 23

THE LEGEND OF ST. GEORGE AND THE DRAGON is a classic tale of good triumphing over evil. A dragon had ravaged the sheep belonging to the people in and around Selena, a city in Libya. When the dragon grew tired of sheep, he demanded a human victim. Lots were drawn and the king's beautiful maiden daughter was chosen. The king offered all his wealth to purchase a substitute, but the people had pledged themselves that no substitutes should be allowed, and so the maiden, dressed as a bride, was led to a marsh to await her fate. The brave knight George was riding by and, after making the sign of the cross, held the dragon at bay by impaling it on his lance. He then borrowed the maiden's girdle (a belt around her waist) and leashed the dragon so the king's daughter could lead him like a lamb.

George was eventually canonized and his emblem, a red cross on a white background, was adopted by Richard The Lionheart and brought to England in the twelfth century. When he became the official saint of England in 1344, that emblem became the national flag, and a day was set aside in his honour.

By the fifteenth century, St. George's Day had become a major feast day in England, almost equivalent to that of Christmas. Even after the Reformation and well into the seventeenth and early eighteenth

The St. George's Society Dinner, Trafalgar Day, Ladies Night, Halifax. Head table guests include: Mr. And Mrs. R.V. Harris. Mr. Harris was president of the society. October 21, 1937.

centuries, it was kept as a holiday of obligation for English Catholics. But, by the 1770s, it was observed by most as a devotional feast, and is now mostly observed by a special dinner.

In Nova Scotia, people of British heritage hold annual dinners to honour the patron saint of the motherland, but the day never did seem to attract the large parades and public gatherings once associated with St. Patrick's Day. (Perhaps that says something about the British reserve.) In any event, members of local St. George's societies around the province gather on April 22 to celebrate the land of their ancestry.

April 23 is also an important day for the Boy Scouts of Canada. St. George is the patron saint of scouting and St. George's Day is when scouts around the world renew their Scout's Promise and of the Scout Law.

Scouts in Nova Scotia have a special reason to be proud. Most scouting historians agree that Port Morion, Cape Breton, had the first Scout troop in Canada—formed less than one year after the original organization was started in England in 1908 by Lord Baden Powell. This feat was highlighted in 1935, when the founder of Scouting made Sydney one of his stopovers on his cross-Canada tour. Scouts from across the province converged in the thousands and the whole town turned out for a huge rally and other celebrations. And you can bet that the flag of St. George was prominently displayed.

IN THE WAY THAT Arbour Day morphed into Earth Day, Secretary's Day has lately been revamped to reflect modern society. Its now beginning to be called Administrative Professional's Day. Although not an official holiday, thanks in part to aggressive promotion by greeting card companies and florists, it has become a well-recognized day in the business and professional world and is now usually called Administrative Professional's Day. Secretary's Day is celebrated on the Wednesday of Professional Secretary's Week, which covers the last full week of April.

Now I would not for a minute say that secretarial personnel don't deserve a holiday—but a whole week? Maybe it's to make up for how poorly paid and ill treated many secretaries used to be. Maybe its to make up for how poorly paid and ill treated some secretaries are today. I'll let the reader be the final judge of that. One thing is certain: the role of the stereotypical secretary is changing. For one thing, larger numbers of men are getting back into the profession.

I say "back into the profession" because years ago it was almost exclusively a man's job. The predecessor of today's secretary was the ancient scribe or clerk. Charles Dickens, who died in 1870, and immortalized his most famous clerk in the persona of Bob Cratchit, probably hadn't known a female clerk.

In the early nineteenth century, the Industrial Revolution changed the way business was carried out. Women and girls joined the ranks of men and boys in low-paying factory jobs. But still, most of the clerical work was done by men. Women's publications of the day didn't advance the cause for female business workers either. The *Ladies Home Journal* of 1900 wrote: "It is a plain, simple fact that women have shown themselves naturally incompetent to fill a great many of the business positions which they have sought to occupy."

Much of that kind of thinking ended by the time World War One was over. In most of the industrialized world, including Nova Scotia, women would come to dominate the clerical field. During the war they filled the gap left by men fighting at the front. When the war

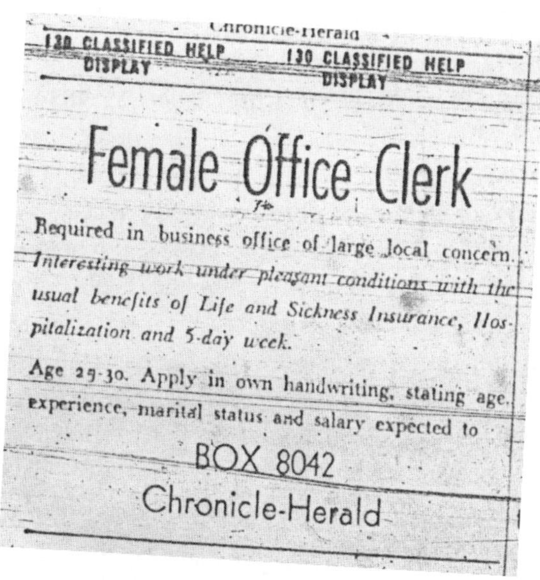
Chronicle-Herald

130 CLASSIFIED HELP DISPLAY — 130 CLASSIFIED HELP DISPLAY

Female Office Clerk

Required in business office of large local concern. *Interesting work under pleasant conditions with the usual benefits of Life and Sickness Insurance, Hospitalization and 5-day week.*

Age 25-30. Apply in own handwriting, stating age, experience, marital status and salary expected to

BOX 8042

Chronicle-Herald

ended, so did many women's jobs, but change had begun. Innovations in the way business needed to be conducted and recorded required expansion and a need for more personnel to handle the paperwork. Since the leaders in the business world felt they needed to keep the wage scale low to meet the demand for a high profit margin, they retained women, who could be paid far less than men. In short, women no longer needed to help in domestic chores were hired to provide cheap labour for the factories and businesses.

Several innovations in machinery and technology also led to the development of a large secretarial pool. Even before the Industrial Revolution was in full swing, methods of taking speedy dictation were being offered to clerks. A man by the name of Bennett placed an advertisement in the October 25, 1832, edition of the *Nova Scotian*, informing the public that "he is the first teacher in the globe who has taught short hand, or as it is called...the winged science, in four lessons." I doubt Bennett was the first teacher in the globe giving dictation lessons and he certainly wasn't the last: Mr. Pitman introduced his method in 1837 and Mr. Gregg began teaching "shorthand" in 1888.

Shorthand was necessary if the secretary was to keep up with the volume of work made possible by the typewriter, which was patented in 1868. Up until World War One, the term typewriter was also used to describe the person operating the machine.

By the latter part of the nineteenth century, women in Nova Scotia were receiving professional training in secretarial skills. In the 1880s the Halifax YWCA began offering women classes in bookkeeping and business English. By the turn of the century, women had entered the workforce in record numbers—albeit at the bottom of the pay scale. As an example, a male clerk at the office of the General Mining Association in Sydney earned $600 per year in 1901—$165 a year above the average miner's wage. A female doing a similar office job would make less than the miner.

In the past few decades we have seen significant changes in the field of secretarial work. Audio recorders have all but eliminated the need for shorthand; typing is now called keyboarding, to reflect the computer skill required by the modern workforce; and women, as well as men, are beginning to be called personal assistants. The term "girl Friday" is no longer acceptable. Even "person-Friday" harks back to a time of servitude. One dictionary defines a secretary as "one entrusted with the secrets and confidences of a superior." One might also say "the backbone of the business industry."

MAY

MAY DAY

MAY 1

In ancient times, spring meant the death of winter and the promise of the return of the earth-warming sun. New life came in the form of budding trees, spring flowers pushing through the late snow, and creatures mating and having offspring. Our ancestors understood that seasonal changes were cyclical, but often believed that the forces making these cycles work had to be appeased and encouraged with offerings and rituals. At winter's end, they held fertility rites and practiced agricultural ceremonies to ensure the season of rebirth would be welcomed back with the respect it deserved. Many of the May Day rites and beliefs that have evolved in the Western world can trace their origins to the Roman festival of Floralia and the Celtic festival of Beltane.

Floralia was a five-day springtime festival held to honour the goddess Flora. The celebrants made offerings of flowers, and welcomed the strengthening sun by ringing bells to ward off the spirits of winter. They encouraged the emerging strength of the sun by lighting votive fires. Spring's fertility was acknowledged by dancing around a budding tree. A maiden was chosen to represent fertility and she presided over the activities.

Similar comparisons can be made with the Celtic festival of Beltane. Ceremonies were held to honour the god of the sun and the rebirth of the earth. A ceremonial queen (often called a May Queen) would be chosen from among the young women of the community and she would rule the day. Some places also selected May Kings. These temporary royals would

wear crowns of flowers and budding branches on their heads. New spring flora was also used to decorate homes. Fairies (both good and bad) were said to be very active on the first day of May, and gifts of food were left on the threshold to keep them appeased. In the evening, bonfires would dot the countryside and people would gather around them to dance and sing. It was a time for couples to pair up and they would be encouraged to leap over the fires or to walk through the smoke to ensure the fertility of their relationship.

Many of these May Day customs have survived, to some degree, into present times. In Italy, where celebrations hark back to those of the festival of Floralia, May 1 is considered the happiest day of the year. In Ireland yellow primroses are sprinkled outside the doorway to protect the home from evil spirits. In Wales a branch of hawthorn is put to similar use. Food offerings survive in Scotland in the form of round breads called bannocks. Often these are marked with a cross and rolled down a hill—if the bannock lands with the cross facing down it is considered bad luck.

For landowners, May Day was also a time for walking the circuit of one's property—known as beating the bounds. It allowed the first spring inspection of winter damage on the land and often involved repairing fences and reestablishing boundary markers. It was a symbolic gesture of marking what is yours with your presence and erecting signs to let others know your claim of ownership. It was also a good time to choose a tree that could serve as a maypole.

The ritual of choosing or erecting a living tree to symbolize fertility is ancient and, many would say, indicative of a primal phallic symbol. Decorating the tree with ribbons to represent the virility of new growth and getting virgin maidens and virile young men to dance around it requires little interpretation of the iconography. For many, May Day, filled with such subliminal and overt fertility rites, was an opportunity to indulge in sexual behaviour that would normally be frowned upon. This licentiousness was one of the reasons Puritan leaders banned May Day celebrations in 1644. They felt there was too much association with pagan beliefs and wanted to turn people away from the traditional spring folk customs. But, while parliaments could enact restrictions, they couldn't totally eradicate traditional beliefs. People continued to celebrate—oftentimes in secret—helping to give rise to the fear that witchcraft was being practised in secret.

With the Restoration in England, the ban on May Day celebrations was lifted and, although a great deal of the overt sexual activities had been suppressed, many of the ceremonies remained in a more gentle form. By the nineteenth century, the Victorians were emphasizing the innocence of May Day festivities. Instead of being a celebration of fertility, it turned into a kind of commemoration of "Merri Olde England." Villagers still gathered around a maypole but, in an age when a piano "leg" was called a limb, few of the symbols would suggest any connection to the graphic phallic icon of their ancestors. A more pastoral, observance-of-nature kind of celebration evolved.

Still, in many places, including Nova Scotia, some remnant of the ancient festivities survived. On Cape Island, children used to go into the woods on May Day morning and dance and sing among the trees. In a hold-over of the tradition of decorating with flowers and budding branches, people in Barrington and elsewhere in the province made May Day baskets from paper or twigs and filled them with flowers to leave on doorsteps or tie to the doorknobs of their friends' homes.

Another May Day ritual widely practised in Nova Scotia was the gathering of May dew. An old British verse gives a clue to the reasoning behind this belief:

The fair maid who, the first of May,
Goes to the field at break of day
And washes in the dew from the hawthorn tree
Will ever after handsome be.

It was both an English and an Acadian custom to collect the dew early on May Day morning and use it on the face to prevent wrinkles. But May water had even more magical powers. In Sister Mary Fraser's twentieth-century collection of folklore from Antigonish and Guysborough counties, titled *Folklore of Nova Scotia*, she tells of the Acadian belief that melted May snow had miraculous power. It was considered a heal-all and was collected and bottled for later use. It could be applied to sores, cuts, bruises, sore throats, and aching ears. Sister Fraser further informs us that it was also used as a substitute for holy water. In addition, it was used by Catholic farmers to anoint cattle and other domestic animals on the morning of May Day. In some cases, this was also the morning when the hairs on the backs of the cattle were singed with a blessed candle to avert the evil eye.

Helen Creighton collected and recorded similar beliefs throughout the province. She also found an example of an old German traditional name for May Day that has associations with the ancient beliefs in good and bad spirits having extra powers on this magical day. At Blandford, she was told that some people called the first day of May "Witch Day," from the German *walpurgis-nacht*—a time for witches to dance away the winter's snow. People were reminded not to borrow or take anything from anybody on that day.

On the first of May, give nothing away.
(Creighton)

INTERNATIONAL WORKER'S DAY

IN MANY COUNTRIES May Day is also officially known as International Worker's Day. It is celebrated by millions around the world as a time to honour the labouring classes. In Canada, Labour Day is the primary holiday to honour workers and is held in September. (See September—Labour Day)

MOTHER'S DAY

Some historians claim that the predecessor of our Mother's Day celebration is the ancient spring festivals dedicated to mother goddesses. In the ancient Greek empire the spring festival honoured Rhea, wife of Cronus and mother of the gods and goddesses. In Rome, the most significant festival similar to Mother's Day was dedicated to the worship of Cybele, another mother goddess. Religious ceremonies in her honour began to be celebrated some time around 250 B.C.

Mother's Day is observed in Canada and the United States on the second Sunday in May, the same as "Mothering Sunday" in Great Britain. This holiday has its origins in the Middle Ages when Christians proclaimed Mothering Sunday to honour Mary, the mother of Christ. The holiday reached its zenith in the medieval period when domestic servants and apprentices were permitted to visit family homes and their mothers. They took with them cakes baked from the scarce supply of sugar and spices. One of the most popular of these was the simnel cake, rich with butter and eggs. Subsequently, the day was also known as Simnel Day.

Special days to honour mothers vary around the world. Norwegians observe Mother's Day on the second Sunday in February; in Lebanon celebrations are held on the first day of spring; in parts of Serbian Yugoslavia, Mother's Day is observed two weeks before Christmas; and in India, Hindus celebrate a ten-day festival in October to honour Durga, the divine mother. The day as we know it in Canada is really a mixture of the British Mothering Sunday and the American celebration introduced after the turn of the twentieth century.

There had been an earlier suggestion in 1872, when Julia Ward Howe (active in the early women's rights movement and best known as the writer of "The Battle Hymn of the Republic") suggested the day be set aside as a day of peace, and a time to remember mothers who had lost sons during the American Civil War. However, a day exclusively set aside to pay tribute to mothers didn't come about until Anna Jarvis of Philadelphia took up the cause in 1907. Devastated when her own mother died on May 9, 1905 (or 1906), Jarvis was determined that the day be set aside in the American calendar to honour motherhood, so she began a letter-writing campaign to clergy, business people, and politicians. Mother Sunday or Mother's Day was first observed on May 10, 1907 (or 1908), in a service in Jarvis's late mother's church in Grafton, West Virginia. The carnation was the flower used in the ceremony as it was her mother's favourite flower. Since then, it is the official flower of Mother's Day—red to honour the living, white for the dead.

Mother's Day is one of those celebrations that is emphasized more by commercial enterprises than by folk traditions. Very few rituals have evolved that are specific to the day. A card and flowers are common, and moms are frequently treated to a dinner out. Many mothers will enjoy (or at least pretend to enjoy) a breakfast in bed lovingly prepared by children and a spouse, many of whom never step into the kitchen except on this special day. An order of burned toast, half-cooked eggs, cold tea, and perhaps some of her own homemade jam may be offered as tangible examples of the love her family feels toward her. Mom will grin, bear it (even eat some of it), and smack her lips. After all, she is a mom!

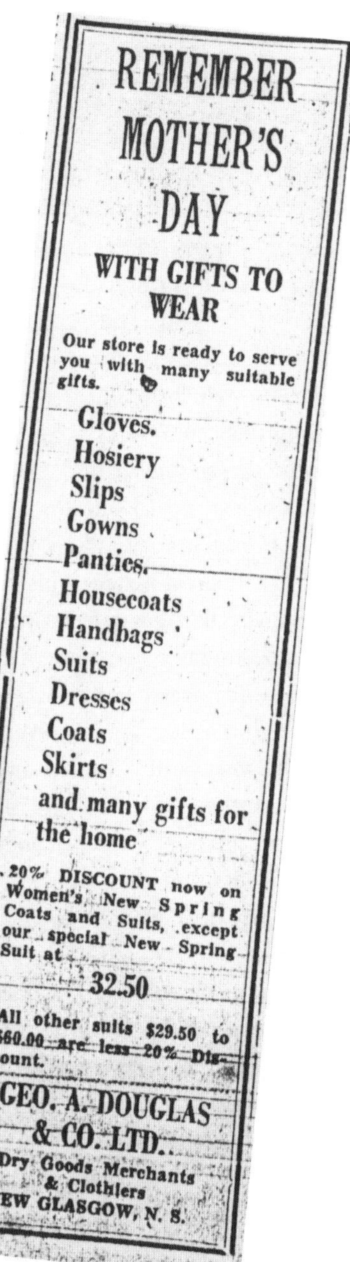

Mother's Day ad, New Glasgow *Eastern Chronicle*, 1950.

VICTORIA DAY

The twenty-forth of May is the Queen's birthday,
If we don't get a holiday, we'll all run away!

VICTORIA DAY IS CANADA'S OLDEST national holiday. But it went through many changes to get to its present state. Before 1845 people in Britain's North American colonies celebrated the reigning monarch's birthday according to the date of the monarch's birth. Each colonial governor could decide whether a public holiday was in order. When Victoria became queen in 1837, her birth date of May 24 was celebrated in much the same way, but in 1845 the date was made an official holiday in Upper and Lower Canada. After Confederation in 1867, Victoria's birthday was officially celebrated every year on the twenty-fourth unless that date was a Sunday, in which case a proclamation was issued providing for a celebration on the twenty-fifth of May.

After Victoria's death in 1901, an act was passed by the Parliament of Canada establishing a legal holiday on May 24 (or May 25, if May 24 fell on a Sunday) under the name Victoria Day. Even though succeeding monarchs' birthdays didn't necessarily fall in May, Victoria Day was recognized as the official time to celebrate them. Canadians continued using this system of choosing the twenty-forth or twenty-fifth for the official holiday until an amendment to the Statutes of Canada in 1952 established the celebration of Victoria Day on the Monday preceding May 25. This moved the date away from being fixed, but ensured Canadians a long weekend each year.

God Bless our Gracious Queen.

On Wednesday last she completed her fourscoure years of life on this terrestrial sphere, honored and beloved by all, regardless of creed or country ; a nation's honor and a nation's pride. On the 24th she began the 81st year of her age ; ten years beyond the alloted time for sojourners in this vale of tears; humanly speaking she may see but a few more days of life here, but let us rest our prayerful hopes, that she will enter into that rest, where pain and sorrow are no more for ever The day was quietly observed in town, but a good time spent by the majority of our folks in the rural districts, and on the banks of our lakes and rivers; but above all, were the flags of our country floating over a free people, never to form a cloak to hide tyranny or slavery.

When the present reining monarch, Elizabeth II, ascended the throne, her official birthday was celebrated according to the rules set up in 1952, even though her actual birth date is in June. And, if you think that's confusing, there's more! In 1957, Victoria Day was permanently designated as the reigning monarch's birthday in Canada, while in the United Kingdom, Queen Elizabeth's birthday is still celebrated in June.

Some senior Canadians may remember a time when May 23 was known as Empire Day. It seems that during the latter years of Queen Victoria's reign, British sentiments were high and people who wanted to hold a special day to honour the empire thought the day before the queen's birthday would be most fitting. In 1898, the Dominion Education Association meeting in Halifax put forward the suggestion that May 23, Empire Day be celebrated in all the provinces' schools. Several provinces, including Nova Scotia, came on board, so for many years school children celebrated Empire Day, although it was not an official holiday. Some people still call Victoria Day "Empire Day"—Canada's oldest holiday, and possibly its most confusing!

Nova Scotians have been celebrating Victoria's holiday in style for years. During the height of the era that bears her name, it was common to meet for parades and games, and in the evening to shoot off fireworks. Boating picnics, bicycle races, and fancy balls were popular. The *British Colonist* of May 25, 1871, describes the day as being "celebrated with military parades, the buildings decked out in bunting, and gun salutes from Citadel Hill and the ships anchored in the harbour." The love and respect most Canadians had for their beloved queen even showed in their term for the pleasant spring weather that they hoped would be in evidence for her holiday. Fine days were frequently said to have enjoyed "Queen's weather." This holiday was especially important for children: the twenty-fourth of May was traditionally the first time they were allowed to go swimming!

JUNE

LIKE MOTHER'S DAY, Father's Day is not an official holiday though it is one celebrated by most North Americans. Its origins are purely American, but its sentiments are universal.

It all began at the turn of the twentieth century. William Smart, an American Civil War veteran, was widowed when his wife died in childbirth, leaving him to raise six children on a rural farm in Washington State. One of his daughters was Sonora Louise Smart Dodd, and when she grew up she looked for a way to honour the love and support her father gave to her and her siblings. In 1909, she proposed a day to honour her father. She chose June because that was his birth month.

The first Fathers' Day celebrations were organized on June 19, 1910, in Spokane, Washington, and Sonora Dodd carried on a long campaign to have the day officially recognized. Her work began to pay off in 1924 when President Calvin Coolidge showed his support for its recognition, but, unfortunately, it wasn't until 1966 that President Lyndon Johnson officially proclaimed the third Sunday in June a national holiday to honour fathers.

Sonora Dodd wasn't alone in her campaign. Harry C. Meek, president of the Lions Club in Chicago, had a hand in establishing Fathers' Day. It seems he gave speeches throughout the United States in support for a day to honour fathers. In 1920 the Lions Clubs of America presented him with a gold watch with the inscription "Originator of Fathers' Day."

Father's Day was celebrated for decades in a quiet way, without much of the commercial hype that came with Mother's Day celebrations. Girls would make their dads cotton pen wipes, embroidered tobacco pouches, or monogrammed handkerchiefs. Boys might carve a new axe handle or cut a new piece of leather for a shaving strap. Commercial cards were less common than those for moms, but one gift remained at the top of the list—if not for the dad, at least for the givers. But really folks, how many neckties can one man own?

If your father is living, wear a red rose.
If your father has passed away, wear a white rose.

J U L Y

CANADA DAY JULY 1

On July 1, 1867, the British North America Act (BNA) proclaimed the formation of a fledgling nation built upon a colonial foundation. With the joining together of Upper and Lower Canada (Ontario and Quebec), New Brunswick, and Nova Scotia, the act described the new country as "one Dominion under the name of Canada." It was that phrasing that helped give a name to the early celebrations marking the anniversaries of the passing of the BNA. But, in typical Canadian fashion, it took a while for most people to agree to the celebration and even to come to terms with what to call the day.

On June 20, 1868, a proclamation signed by the governor general, Lord Monck, called upon Her Majesty's subjects throughout the Dominion to join in the celebration of the anniversary of the formation of Canada. But, it wasn't until twenty-two years after Confederation, in 1879, that Parliament officially named the anniversary Dominion Day. And for many people it still wasn't a day for rejoicing.

Many Nova Scotians saw Confederation as the ruin of their beloved province. In most communities, including my hometown of Sherbrooke, anti-Confederationists draped their homes in black crepe and wore mourning armbands to protest the loss of Nova Scotia's independence. These feelings took a long time to die down, and in some cases lasted well

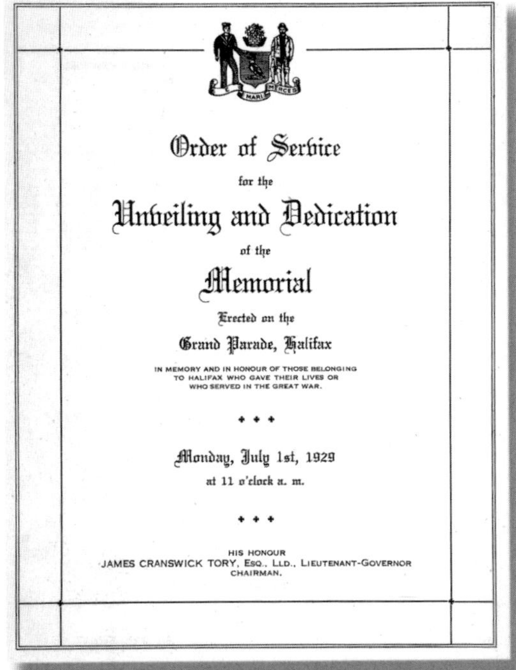

Order of Service
for the
Unveiling and Dedication
of the
Memorial
Erected on the
Grand Parade, Halifax

IN MEMORY AND IN HONOUR OF THOSE BELONGING TO HALIFAX WHO GAVE THEIR LIVES OR WHO SERVED IN THE GREAT WAR.

* * *

Monday, July 1st, 1929
at 11 o'clock a. m.

* * *

HIS HONOUR
JAMES CRANSWICK TORY, ESQ., LLD., LIEUTENANT-GOVERNOR
CHAIRMAN.

Order of Service for the unveiling of the cenotaph at the Grand Parade, Halifax, July 1, 1929.

into the twentieth century. An editorial statement in the *Acadian Recorder*, July 1, 1885 read: "you don't see any flag up at my place today, do you?...it was a bad day for Nova Scotia when the cause for Dominion Day came about."

Depending on which government was in power in the first few decades after Confederation, Dominion Day celebrations ranged from scant to non-existent. In the nineteenth century, when the Liberals were in office in Nova Scotia, Dominion Day proclamations were often not issued. Schoolhouses in Dartmouth, Halifax, and elsewhere were frequently kept open on the first of July. If a school board did choose to give the children a holiday, it risked losing its government grant unless it made up the day later.

The idea of Nova Scotia leaving Confederation was a hot political topic.

In the election campaign of 1886, Premier W. S. Fielding and his Liberal party swept into power with the slogan "Secession," and as late as the 1920s the Maritime Rights Movement organized to secede. But even with the Fielding government advocating taking Nova Scotia out of Confederation, by the 1890s Dominion Day celebrations were drawing huge crowds.

One such celebration in the Annapolis Valley was described in the July 2, 1896, edition of the *Morning Chronicle*. The paper's reporter noted the current craze for anything to do with bicycles, including a grand bicycle parade that started in Windsor and ran up through the Valley. The report concluded: "The celebration at Bridgetown today (July 1) was very largely attended. It being estimated that there were over 4000 persons in town, the chief attraction was the races...the band of the 69th Battalion was present and discoursed some choice music. A bicycle procession paraded the principal streets in the morning. Everything passed off satisfactorily."

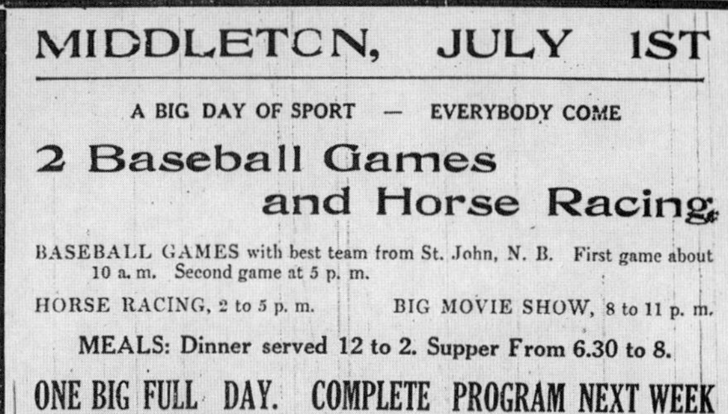

MIDDLETCN, JULY 1ST
A BIG DAY OF SPORT — EVERYBODY COME
2 Baseball Games
and Horse Racing
BASEBALL GAMES with best team from St. John, N. B. First game about 10 a. m. Second game at 5 p. m.
HORSE RACING, 2 to 5 p. m.
BIG MOVIE SHOW, 8 to 11 p. m.
MEALS: Dinner served 12 to 2. Supper From 6.30 to 8.
ONE BIG FULL DAY. COMPLETE PROGRAM NEXT WEEK

Isn't that a great Canadian sentiment? "Everything passed off satisfactorily." Either the reporter's (and the newspaper's) sentiments were with the anti-Confederationists, or the report was an early display of our modest Canadian national pride.

There was, apparently, not much in the line of organized ceremonies on a federal scale until the fiftieth anniversary of Confederation in 1917, when the new Centre Block of the Parliament Buildings, under construction in Ottawa, was dedicated as a memorial to the Fathers of Confederation and to honour Canadians fighting in the terrible "War to end all Wars" in Europe. Ten years later, in 1927, in

Float decorated for Canada's Diamond Jubilee, Fort Anne, Annapolis Royal, 1927.

recognition of Canada's Diamond Jubilee, the governor general in Ottawa laid the cornerstone of the Confederation Building, and the Carillon was rung for the first time from the Peace Tower. Helen Creighton, then a young writer working out of Ottawa, published a patriotic piece about these bells. She suggested Canada had come of age musically, writing: "Canadians…(are) qualifying themselves now to take their place among the great music-loving nations of the world." It would seem that even if the governments weren't taking up the cause of national pride, writers and artists were trying to wave the flag whenever they could.

After World War One, and the depression that followed, many people looked to holidays for an escape. By 1935 numerous Dominion Day celebrations were taking place all over Nova Scotia: there was a Dominion Day golf tournament at the Gorsebrook Golf Club in Halifax, and thousands of Boy Scouts and Girl Guides attended a special rally in Sydney with their founder Lord Baden-Powell; on the Dartmouth Lakes and at the Jubilee Boat Club on Halifax's Northwest Arm, regattas and decorated boat parades, followed in the evening by flotillas of big and small crafts with lanterns, marked the day. At Middleton, Dominion Day horse races drew huge crowds.

So, it seems that despite any major concerted effort on the part of the federal government, Canadians were creating their own celebrations. National pride and interest in celebrating things Canadian grew stronger during and after World War Two, and since 1958 the government has arranged official Dominion Day celebrations under the charge of the Secretary of State. These revelries reached a new height during Canada's centennial celebrations which were followed with large-scale affairs from Parliament Hill and in the provinces and territories.

This growth of national identity also helped fuel a desire by many to change the name of the holiday. For many people, the term Dominion, which derived from the BNA, seemed to imply ties with Britain. Many Canadians were looking to express their independence and naming their official birthday holiday after the nation seemed one way to accomplish this. On October 27, 1982, the holiday once known as Dominion Day officially became known as Canada Day, which is always observed on the first day of July unless that date falls on a Sunday, in which case it is observed the following Monday.

Today, Canadians celebrate the anniversary of the founding of their country with renewed vigor. Parties, parades, fireworks, nationally televised concerts, and gatherings of family and friends mark the day. Canadian flags are waved and painted on faces—it's almost safe to say we have lost some of our reserve.

ST. SWITHIN'S DAY JULY 15

For Nova Scotians living in the eighteenth and nineteenth centuries, St. Swithen's Day was a demarcation day for weather watchers. Farmers especially watched the skies for signs of rain and harked back to the traditions surrounding this customary divination day.

A councillor of Egbert, King of Wessex, Saint Swithin lived in the ninth century. Ten years after being appointed bishop of Winchester in 852 A.D., he died. He was buried outside the north wall of his Cathedral, as he had requested—he wanted passers-by to be able to walk on his grave, and he also hoped the rain from the roof of the cathedral would drip down on his bones. Years after his internment, church officials had those bones removed to the sanctuary, which apparently displeased the saint to no end. A folk rhyme developed around the divination attributes of his bones. One of the most common variants is:

St. Swithin's day, if thou dost rain,
For forty days it will remain;
St. Swithin's day, if thou be fair,
For forty days will rain nae mair.

Another belief concerning rain on St. Swithen's Day is that it is caused by St. Mary Magdalene washing her handkerchief to go to St. James' Fair. A version of this belief, found in Nova Scotia at Whynaught's Settlement by Helen Creighton, is: if Mary goes over the hill and gets her skirts wet it will rain for forty days.

FESTIVAL OF ST. ANNE

ALTHOUGH THIS CELEBRATION is primarily observed in Nova Scotia by the Mi'kmaq, its roots go back so far and have been shared over so many years by non-natives that it is recognized as a blended traditional celebratory day. This holiday is a fascinating Canadian example of the merging of two major belief systems: traditional Mi'kmaw spiritualism and Christianity. St. Anne, the mother of the Virgin Mary, is the patron saint of the Catholic Mi'kmaq. In Nova Scotia, the ceremonies held to honour her and celebrate the Mi'kmaw way of life is most evident at Chapel Island, in Cape Breton.

People have been writing about the event since the 1890s, but many of the early accounts denigrated the native ceremonies and ways of life, and dismissed their traditional spiritualism in favor of European concepts. By the turn of the twentieth century, a more unbiased picture of the celebrations began to emerge. The July 29, 1901, issue of the *Sydney Post* reported that the St. Anne's Day celebrations were initially held each year on July 26, but added: "it is the custom to postpone the celebration of this feast till the following Sunday." The paper reported that around one thousand people attended the various religious and

St. Anne's Day Procession, July 26, 1930, Chapel Island.

secular ceremonies, and that two steamers conveyed passengers from Sydney, while an additional ferry brought celebrants from Baddeck and Arichat.

Dr. Elsie Clews Parsons, an American anthropologist who conducted research into Mi'kmaw culture in the early years of the twentieth century and published her findings in the *Journal of American Folklore*, described a visit she made to observe the Chapel Island festivities in 1923. On approaching the island, she saw one large cross and the ten stations of the cross marked by smaller crosses running up a cleared trail. Many of the celebrants had erected wigwams, the majority of which were made with tar paper or canvas instead of the traditional birchbark. Over the multi-day event, numerous Catholic services were conducted, with the main event being on Sunday. After a mass in the morning and a mid-day meal, the celebrants made a procession before statues of the Virgin Mary and St. Anne up to an iron cross set in a boulder. Later, some devotees took part in a ceremony known as "Crawling to St. Anne's." Beginning on their knees at the door of the chapel, they crawled up the aisle to the altar. Dr. Parsons was told that in order to be cured of an illness, one had to have "a strong heart and a pure heart...by going to see St. Anne on your knees." Later in the day a dinner was held followed by dancing and singing.

A similar festival was held at the other end of the province at Bear River, reaching its zenith in the 1930s, but continuing for years after. Hundreds of Mi'kmaq and non-natives attended. Celebrants dressed in native costumes and participated in traditional dances and sports.

Today's festival at Chapel Island has become a celebration of traditional Mi'kmaw and Christian beliefs, but it is also a time for First Nations peoples from across the Maritimes to gather and reaffirm their sovereignty and fellowship.

AUGUST

CIVIC HOLIDAY

THE FIRST MONDAY OF AUGUST is celebrated as a civic holiday in all Canadian provinces and territories, except Quebec and Newfoundland. In small communities, celebrations usually included a parade of business, trade, and civic officials, and various forms of public participation aimed at celebrating the local history and natural resources of the area. While some towns and villages still celebrate in this way, its now more common to see the August civic holiday as the one set aside to allow as many people as possible to have a long weekend.

Celebrations have changed over the past few decades, and they will continue to evolve depending on the popular tastes of the day and the people organizing the events. One need only look at how Nova Scotia's capital city, Halifax, celebrated its annual civic holiday to see how styles of festivities have evolved. In 1999 Halifax celebrated the 250th anniversary of its founding. While most Natal Day celebrations took place in June, Haligonians still enjoyed the August civic holiday, playing both sides of the fence and getting in double the amount of party time! But, if we look back at how the capital city celebrated its milestone anniversaries, we can get some idea of the scope and styles of civic festivities popular throughout the centuries.

One might be tempted to think the Victorian citizens who celebrated Halifax's one hundredth birthday might have done so with reserve and refined teas. Not so! According to various reports in the June 1849 issues of the *Nova Scotian*, Haligonians celebrated with the style of true partygoers. The party began with the firing of one hundred cannon shots beginning at 4:00 A.M. This noisy display was followed by all the city's bells pealing to rouse anyone who happened to sleep through the cannon volleys. Then, at 10:00 A.M., the troops were led out onto the Grand Parade (a public square in downtown Halifax) where they were reviewed by the lieutenant governor, Sir John Harvey. After the troops were reviewed, they participated in a sham battle.

Next was one of the most popular events: the grand parade! A procession of Mi'kmaw representatives, local statesmen, and dignitaries left the Grand Parade and moved on to Citadel Hill for a twenty-one gun salute. The parade was a mile long, included five thousand marchers, and took sixty-five minutes to pass. One of the most interesting features in the procession was a horse-drawn carriage which held Joseph Howe's famous printing press. As it moved through the crowd, copies of a special poem written by the elder statesman and newspaper editor were printed off and distributed to the crowd. For those who didn't get a copy, Beamish Murdock, noted lawyer and recorder for the city of Halifax, treated the crowds to his reading of the poem. Titled "Hail to the Day," it reflected the popular concepts of loyalty and strong ties to Britain. The first verse proclaimed:

All hail the day when Britons came over
And planted their standard, with sea-foam still wet'
Around and above us their spirits will soar
Rejoicing to mark how we honour it yet.

J. POWER & SON
THEY COME
first trades possession of Dartmouth N.S. Aug 4th 1898
Outside 85 Portland Street the float of John Power & Son in the first Natal Day industrial parade
[Natal Day celebrations started in 1895 with an afternoon and evening program only.) Standing left to right Frank Greene, John Hughes
Frank Power, Thomas A Morash, blacksmith; James MacDougall, wood worker, James Baker (hand on wheel) John Power in felt hat. Driver and man
alongside unidentified. Garrett Kingston and Alexander Hutt were the other two carriage builders in Dartmouth at this time.
The building shown here had been the barn and carriage house of Dominick Farrell who owned the present Owl Drugstore property
& lived there. Sleighs used to be stored in the carriage house in summer.

First trades procession of Dartmouth, August 4, 1898. Outside 85 Portland Street, the float of John Power & Sons in the 1st Natal Day Industrial Parades 1898. [Natal Day started in 1895 with an afternoon and evening program] L-R: Frank Greene; John Hughes, carriage painter; Frank Power; Thomas A. Morash, blacksmith; James MacDougall, wood worker; James Baker [hand on wheel]; John Power [in felt hat]. Driver and man alongside unidentified.

The Provincial Building was decorated with a beautiful arch that spanned the street and featured a novelty—gas lights, while on the public commons, the first post of the new electric telegraph was erected.

Throughout the city military bands played and the evening was capped with a fireworks display in the harbour.

One hundred years later, Halifax was once again ready for a major civic party. The port city was just coming out of the dreariness of World War Two in 1949 when it celebrated its bicentennial anniversary. Civic officials saw it as an opportunity to pull out all the stops. The *Halifax Chronicle* published a special bicentennial issue in June, copies of which could be mailed

Halifax Bicentennial Parade on Quinpool Road, 1949.

to friends outside the province for four cents. For those interested in the early history of the city, reporters and local historians gave some fascinating tidbits, including an item informing residents that, in Halifax's early days, young women employed in the washing trade used to gather at the governor's pasture near Africville to wash their clothes and lay them on the grassy fields to dry.

Bicentennial organizers planned a thirteen-week celebration program that included church services, band concerts, the crowning of Miss Halifax, a "monster" Natal Day parade, international baseball games on the Commons, a concert by Miss Portia White, and regattas on the water, topped with a Venetian evening featuring decorated boats and lanterns on the Northwest Arm.

As a souvenir of the bicentennial, residents could visit Mills Brothers and for $6.98 buy a silk scarf from Paris printed with images of Halifax's most famous landmarks.

Premier Angus L. Macdonald wrote a lengthy article in the paper extolling Halifax's virtues, while proclaiming a new vision for the city. Post-war Halifax was not known for its beauty, and Premier Macdonald wanted to enlist the help of citizens to change this. He wrote: "Halifax is sometimes criticized for dinginess, for untidy streets and homes...[I] should like to see Halifax become known as the cleanest city in Canada!"

While the centennial and bicentennial celebrations show how the capital city of Nova Scotia celebrated its major civic holidays, thousands of smaller civic festivities were held in towns and villages in every county. And, while pride of place is still obvious, many organizers are now looking to bring focus to their community for economic reasons. As a result, some civic holidays are more like trade fairs. It will be interesting to see where our August civic holiday goes over the next few decades. Will it be a time to celebrate and reflect on the history and culture of a region, or merely another summer holiday to escape to the beach and enjoy a barbecue with friends? Only time will tell.

ACADIAN DAY

AUGUST 15

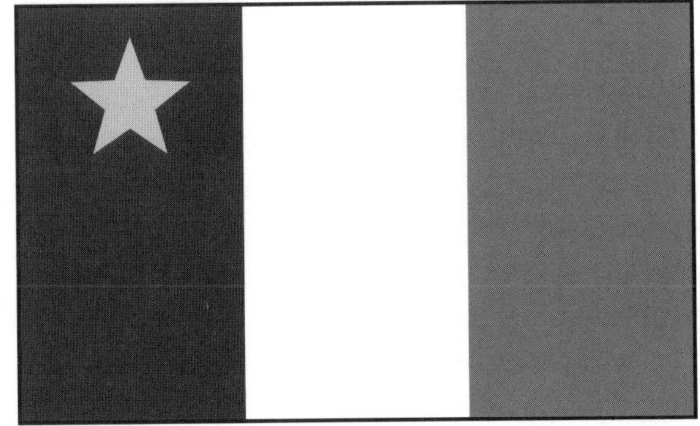

Nova Scotia, the land, and its people have had a varied and exciting history. Why, even the name we use for the geographic locality we inhabit has gone through many changes. The indigenous people called the region *Mi'kmaqui* and the British used the Latin version for New Scotland. But, had the tides of history been reversed, we may know our land as "Acadie," the lands of the Acadians.

In 1524, Giovanni Verrazano, a Florentine adventurer in the service of François I of France, visited our Atlantic shores and named the area "Arcadie," from the ancient province in Greece fabled for its beautiful trees and pastoral landscapes. Over the centuries, map makers changed or misspelled the word until it became "Acadia."

Another explanation suggests the name is either a corruption of the Maliseet word *quoddy* meaning a fertile place, or the Mi'kmaw word *algatig*, meaning a camp site. In fact a number of places in the land of the Acadians end in "quoddy" or "acadie," such as Shubenacadie, Tracadie, and Passamaquoddy.

A third theory for the etymology of the term "Acadia" argues it comes from Scotland. Many people claim Prince Henry and his band of men from the Orkney Islands were some of the first Europeans to settle in Nova Scotia in 1398, albeit for a short time. Henry Sinclair's Earldom of Orkney was then called "orchadie." Could the name of his lands in Scotland be the origin? The debate continues. It does seem clear, however, that the early French settlers to Nova Scotia were familiar and comfortable with the term Acadia, and it is that name and their heritage that are celebrated each August 15.

Every school child in Nova Scotia should be familiar with the story of the expulsion of the Acadians in 1755. The national historic site at Grand Pré illustrates that unfortunate time in our history very well. But, after the Acadians began to make their way back to the land of their birth, a renewed urgency to re-establish themselves as a strong cultural force emerged. Over the years, this urgency saw fruition in political and social action, including choosing their own special feast day.

Richard Family reunion 1991. The author's mother-in-law, Marjorie (Richard) Campagna, is second from left, top row.

In 1881, the Acadians, under the direction of the Catholic bishops of the Maritime Provinces, went against most of the other francophones in Canada, who held their feast day on June 24 (the feast of St. John) and officially adopted August 15, the feast of the Assumption, as the day to celebrate Acadian life and culture. They also adopted their own hymn, *Ave Marie Stella*. Sung in Latin, this hymn had been a rallying song for Acadians since about 1630. (For the music see *Folksongs of the Maritimes* by Kaye Pottie and Vernon Ellis, page 119.)

Ave, maris stella,
Dei Mater alma,
Atque semper virgo,
Felix coeli porta,
Felix coeli porta.
Amen.

Star of sea, we hail thee,
Hail God's Mother, kindly,
Thou eternal virgin,
Blessed gate of heaven,
Blessed gate of heaven.
Amen.

But the most visible symbol of Acadian pride must be the tri-colour flag with the bright yellow star. The flag was chosen in Miscouche, Prince Edward Island, in 1884, during the Second National Acadian Congress. It was proposed by Reverend Marcel-François Richard from Saint-Louis, New Brunswick. Richard reminded the assembly that the tri-coloured flag is France's flag, and since Acadians are descendants of that French heritage, the flag has the right to fly throughout the entire world according to international laws. He wanted the Acadian flag not only to remind people of their European heritage, but also to represent their strong North American/French roots. For that reason, a yellow star, representing the star of Mary, Stella Maris, would serve as a distinct Acadian icon in the flag. The original Acadian flag was made by Marie Babinda, a schoolteacher in Saint-Louis, New Brunswick. It can be seen at University de Moncton's Acadian museum.

So, for years, Acadians have been flying their flag and celebrating their heritage and culture, especially on August 15. The day is most often marked by a mass, often followed by a community meal and heritage activities. It is a time to remember those who came before and to renew the spirit of Acadie. An editorial in the August 15, 1946, edition of the Acadian newspaper *Le Petit Courrier* put the sentiments into perspective beautifully: "C'est aujourd'hui notre fête. Quel encouragement, quelles belles leçons de patriotisme et quelle forte inspiration ne peut-on pas retirer dans ce simple exercise de l'esprit! Faisons-le aujourd'hui. C'est un acte de reconnaissance que nous devons à nos Pères, eux qui ont beaucoup plus mérité de la vie que nous. Et il nous fera du bien ca pèlerinage en esprit en ce our de notre patronne, la fête de l'Assomption." (Tomorrow is our Holiday. What encouragement, what beautiful lessons of patriotism, and what strong inspiration are drawn from this simple practice of the spirit. Celebrate tomorrow. It is an act of remembrance that we must do for our forefathers, those who were much more deserving of that life than we. This pilgrimage will do us so much good, in heart and soul, for our celebration of L'Assomption.)

SEPTEMBER

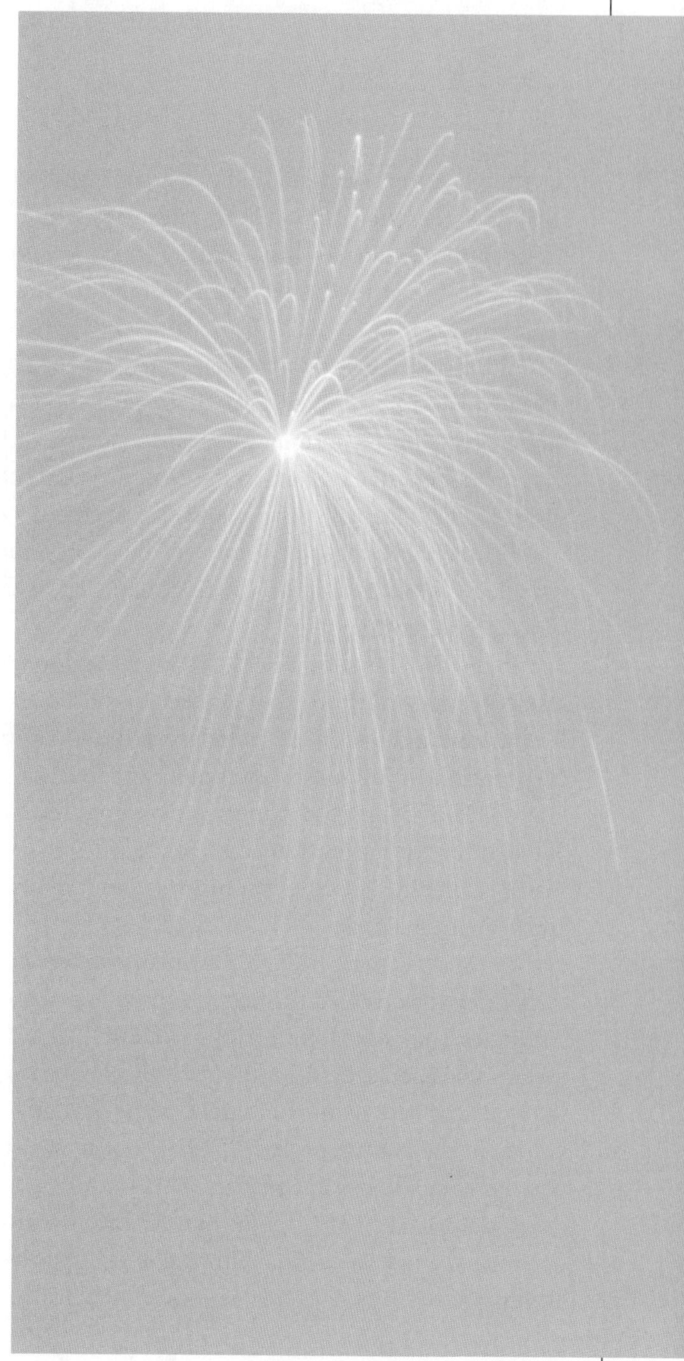

Labour Day in Canada shouldn't be confused with May Day (or International Workers' Day), which is held on the first day of May in many countries, with the exception of the United States, South Africa, and Canada.

In Canada, Labour Day is celebrated on the first Monday in September and, like many other holidays and celebrations, its origins are in dispute. American labour leaders make claim to the first such celebration, while Canadian sources hold firm to the belief that Labour Day originated north of the forty-ninth parallel. I'll toss my hat on the Canadian side of the line and present my case.

In the United States, Peter J. McGuire, the founder and general secretary of the United Brotherhood of Carpenters and one of the founders of the American Federation of Labour is known as the "father of Labour Day." There is, however, some suggestion that he got his idea from Canadian trade unionists in 1882, a decade after the first major attempt to organize labour in Canada.

Ten years earlier, in 1872, Canadian workers held what might be termed the first unofficial Labour Day activities. They were fighting for a freedom that today seems inalienable, but back then was illegal: the right to form and be a member of a trade union. Britain had repealed the anti-union law in 1871, but it was still on the statute books in Canada.

On April 15, 1872, the Toronto Trades Assembly organized a demonstration and parade in support of twenty-four imprisoned leaders of the Toronto Typographical Union, on strike to try to secure a shorter (nine-hour) working day. A parade of labourers marched down the streets, accompanied by four marching bands. They were watched by at least ten thousand Torontonians.

A similar demonstration was held that same year in Ottawa on September 3 when members of seven labour unions organized a huge parade. The marchers went to the home of the prime minister, Sir John A. MacDonald, where they hoisted him into a carriage and drew him to Ottawa City Hall. Canada's founding father promised support for the unionist cause and vowed to "sweep away all such barbarous laws from the statute books." Whether out of astute political bargaining or his government's genuine interest in reform, the restriction against trade unions was repealed by the Canadian government by the end of the year.

Ten years later, in 1882, the Toronto Trades and Labour Council (the former Toronto Trades Association) was organizing their annual demonstration and picnic for July 22, and sent an invitation to New York, inviting Peter J. McGuire to be their guest speaker. Later that year, Mr. McGuire instigated the first organized labour picnic and demonstration in New York City on September 5. He even suggested a name for the celebration: Labour Day. Clearly inspired by what he had observed in Toronto, Peter McGuire may be the American progenitor of Labour Day, but his baby was conceived in Canada.

The labour movement continued to grow in both

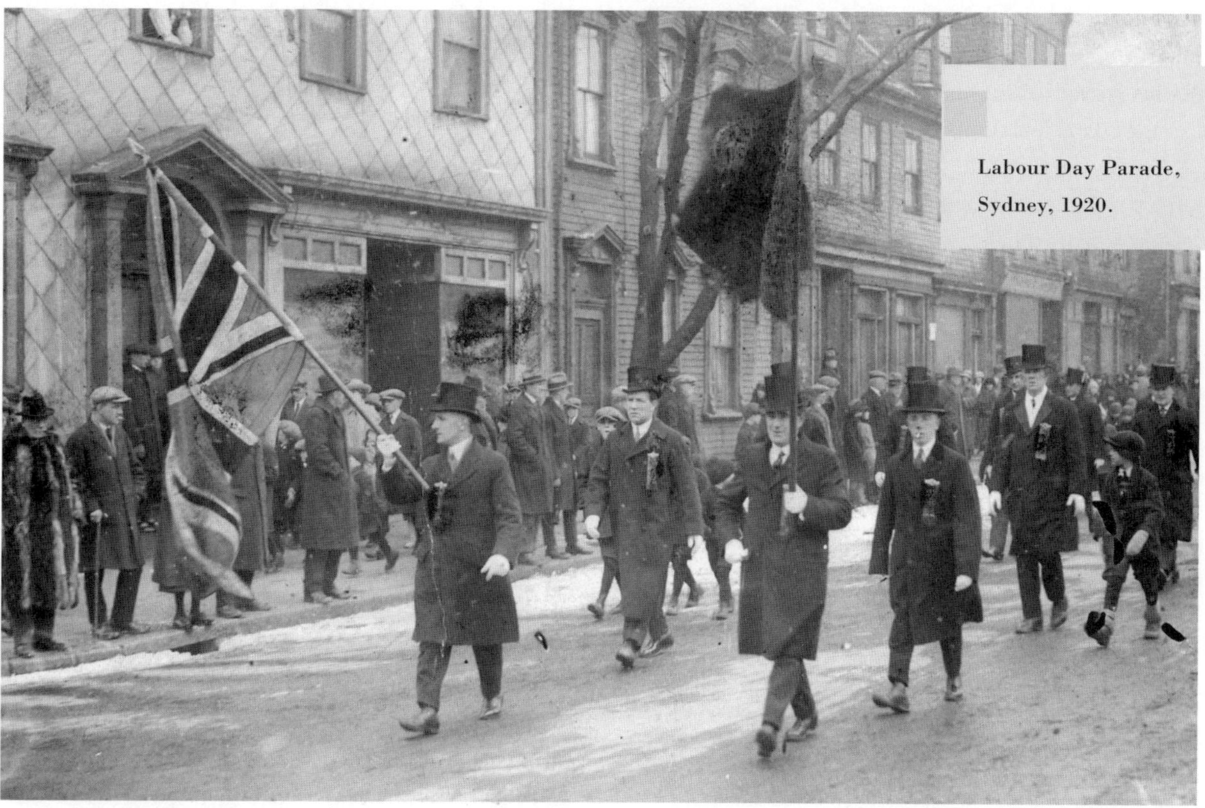

Labour Day Parade, Sydney, 1920.

the United States and Canada. Canadian activists began lobbying for an official national holiday and, on July 23, 1894, the federal government of Sir John Sparrow Thompson declared Labour Day a national holiday. The celebrations occurred on various dates, but, finally in the late 1890s, the holiday was moved to the first Monday in September.

Prime Minister Thompson, who was born in Nova Scotia, was familiar with workers' disputes and the attempts of organized labour to unionize in his own province. Many labour unions took their roots from the various benefit societies connected to international workers organizations and cultural groups (such as the Charitable Irish Society) present in Nova Scotia in the 1800s. In 1879 in Springhill, the Provincial Workman's Association was formed in response to the poor conditions in the mines. And, even before 1894, when the holiday was made official, Nova Scotia's *Acadian Recorder* of August 2, 1888, reported the first Labour Day celebrations being held in Halifax.

Three years later, in its July 23, 1891 edition, the same paper reported on a huge Labour Day parade and related activities held two days earlier on the Halifax Commons. (The holiday was supposed to be held on the twentieth, but was postponed because of rain.) There were hundreds of union workers, watched by thousands of spectators. Marchers included representatives from the police force, workers from the pressmen's association, shipwrights and caulkers, the fire corps, carpenters, and many other trades and businesses. A vivid description of the attire of some of the members of the typographical union brings the scene to life:

> *The compositors turned out 70 active men strong, in silk hats, white ties and gloves, and wore pretty blue silk badges, trimmed with silver; each had a bouquet, and variety was added to the pleasing black clothes and shining ties by the red sashes of the officers and their beautiful banners of the Union on which was announced superrogatively that 'The Press is the light of the world.'*

Later in the day, over one thousand of the participants boarded boats and sailed to McNab's Island in Halifax Harbour for a Labour Day picnic.

Not all communities were so labour conscious. In Cape Breton, The *Sydney Post* of July 29, 1901, reported

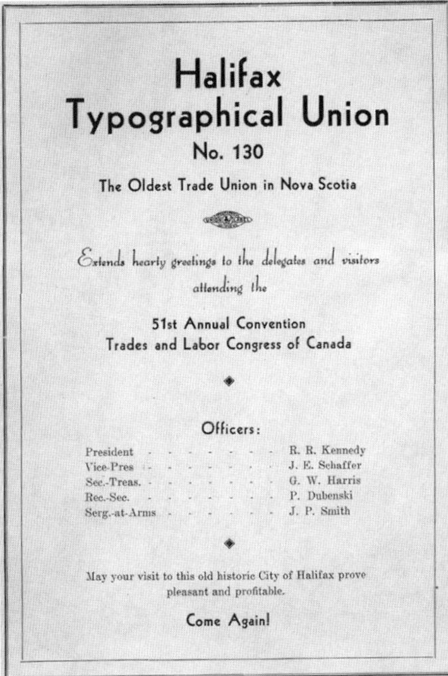

Ad for the Halifax Typographical Union #130—the oldest Trade Union in Nova Scotia.

on discussions by leaders as to whether holding a celebration for Labour Day seemed a good idea, given the sentiments of the mine workers and their ties to labour. Fears of labour ties to socialist (already being called Bolshevist) causes were evident. Still, over the years, some aspects of Nova Scotia's labour movements made headway. The provincial government adopted the Trade Unions Act in 1937, the first such act adopted by any province, which stated that a company cannot arbitrarily ignore the existence of a worker's union.

So, although the struggle goes on, with all parties claiming victories and crying foul, Labour Day is one tangible way of acknowledging the importance of the contribution of workers. And when you're enjoying that long weekend or closing up the cottage, perhaps raise a glass to the workers—after all, they're you and me!

OCTOBER

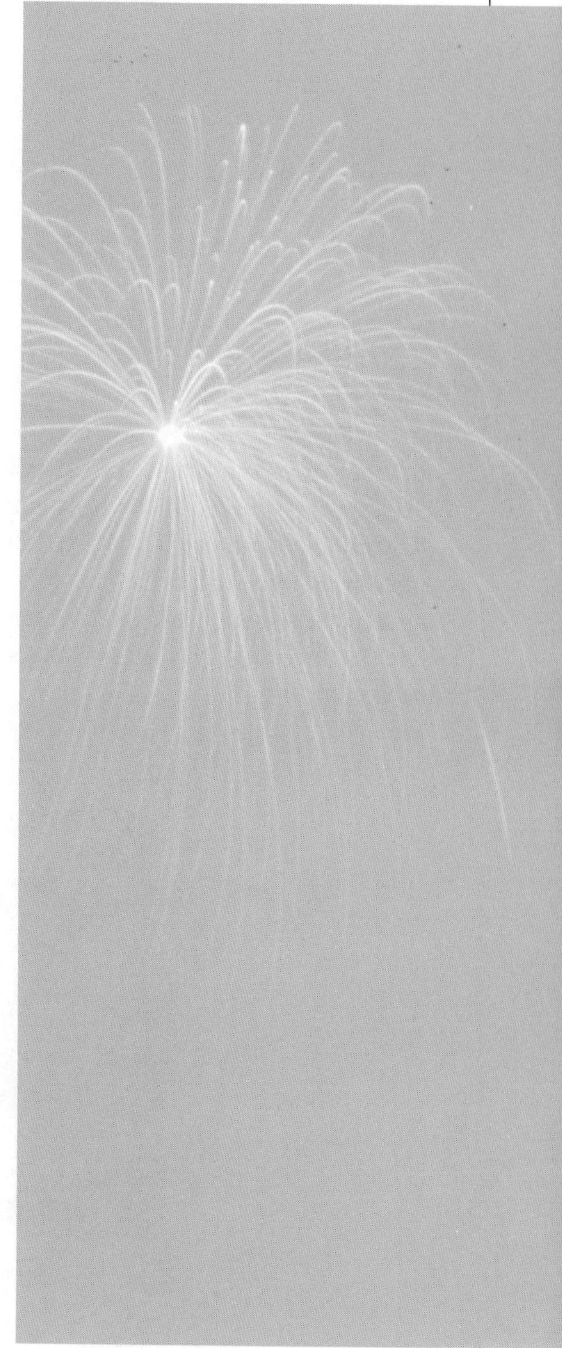

WHILE THE CANADIAN AND AMERICAN thanksgiving celebrations may seem similar, they have distinct differences both in custom and origin. The American celebrations focus on the early New England pilgrims and their relationship with the native people. Their traditions (including the foods served) revolve around the autumnal harvest which, in Canada, usually occurs in October as opposed to November in many of the southern American states. The Canadian version of Thanksgiving has quite different origins.

Early government officials in British North America used to proclaim special days of thanksgiving to mark (among other things) a successful expedition, a discovery, a victorious battle, a treaty, or the recovery from illness of a royal personage. In Nova Scotia, some of these early celebrations included a day of thanksgiving on October 10, 1710, to celebrate the British capture of Port Royal from the French, and another in 1763, when the citizens of Halifax celebrated a general day of thanksgiving after the signing of the Treaty of Paris which gave Canada to Britain. Beginning with the New England Planters in 1759, and then, during and after the American Revolutionary War with the United Empire Loyalists, settlers from the American colonies brought many of their thanksgiving harvest traditions north. But still, no formal declaration of a fall thanksgiving day was made.

Even without a formal declaration, Nova Scotians still found ways to express their thanksgiving

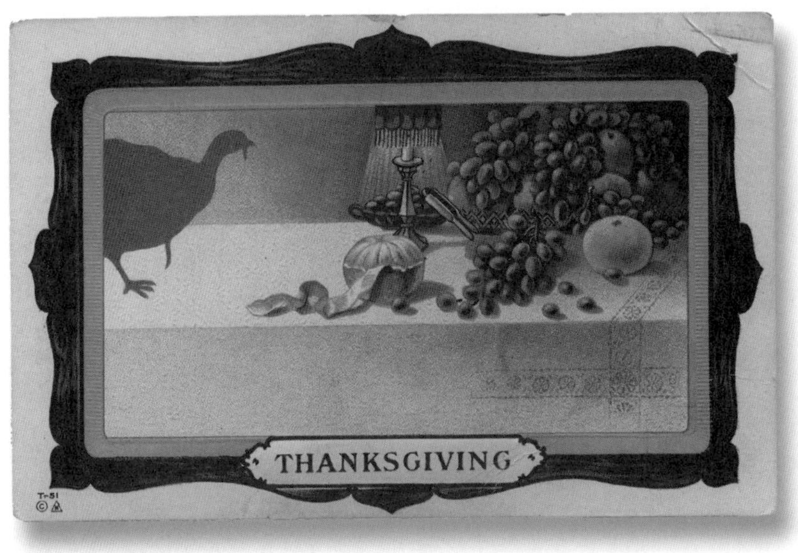

emotions. The following may be Nova Scotia's first published thanksgiving poem. It was written by Joseph Howe in 1868:

Almighty Father at Thy Throne
A grateful people kneel,
Father of Mercies, Thou alone
Canst compass what we feel.
In prayer and praise our souls ascend
To Thy Almighty Throne;
Father of Mercies—guide and friend
Our humble tribute own.

We thank Thee for the stars above,
The flow'ry soil we tread,
For friendship's grasp—the smile of love,
The song bird overhead,
And for the hallow'd life and death
Of Him to guide us given:
The hopes that hang upon His breath,
The promised rest in Heaven.

We thank Thee for the daily bread
That human life sustains;
For flocks and herds profusely spread
O'er all our hills and plains,
For lesser mercies teach us too
The grateful song of praise:
Let all we think, and say, and do,
Be molded to Thy praise.

(Note: Years later, in 1973, the poem was set to music by Trevor Jones for the first Joseph Howe Festival in Halifax. See Nova Scotia Archives and Records Management, MG 1, Volume 5 #13.)

What may be considered the first official Thanksgiving Day for Canada was observed after Confederation, on April 15, 1872, to celebrate the recovery of the Prince of Wales (later King Edward VII) from a serious illness. The prince's mother, Queen Victoria, proclaimed a British day of prayer and thanksgiving for the recovery of her son. Naturally, Canada joined in.

There seems to be no official government record of a formal declaration of a day of thanksgiving between 1872 and 1878, but in 1879 Thanksgiving Day became a national day of observance in Canada. From 1879 to 1898 it was observed on a Thursday in November. In 1899, it was moved to a Thursday in October, where it stayed until 1907, with the exception of 1901 and 1904 when the date was moved back to a Thursday in November. Then, from 1908 to 1921, it was observed on a Monday in October, the exact date being appointed by proclamation. Try to keep up—it gets even more confusing!

In 1921 the Government of Canada issued the ruling: "The holiday commonly called Thanksgiving Day being a day usually appointed in the month of October or November, by proclamation as a day of general thanksgiving to Almighty God, shall whenever appointed be proclaimed for and on Armistice Day." So, from 1921 to 1930 the two days were celebrated together. This changed in 1931 when the days were separated into two unique holidays. And, finally, in 1957, Parliament announced that on the second Monday in October, Thanksgiving would be "a day of general thanksgiving to almighty God for the bountiful harvest with which Canada has been blessed."

Good thing too! After all, Canadians had been celebrating a form of harvest Thanksgiving Day for years. Churches were decorated with fall leaves and the produce of the fields. We even adopted the custom of a family meal and, especially after World War Two, made sure that turkeys were the centrepiece of the feast. In fact, a small note in the December 3, 1898, edition of the *Presbyterian Witness* is evidence that Nova Scotians were serving up turkey and celebrating Thanksgiving well before the government made it official: "A family in Yarmouth procured a Thanksgiving turkey from the market, it cost 90 cents, but when they began to prepare it they found in the gizzard four ten cent pieces and a five cent piece." Now, that's something to be thankful for.

INTERNATIONAL BOSS'S DAY   OCTOBER 16

HERE IS ANOTHER HOLIDAY that has only become popular in the past decade. I have included it because, like Secretary's Day (or Administrative Professional's Day), it has reached a certain popularity with the public due to the popular media and the commercial hype associated with it. After all, if bosses can be made guilty by clever marketing to fête their helpers with a special day, surely the lowly workers can reciprocate with a similar day of honour. It will be interesting to see where this holiday goes in relation to tradition and custom. I think it's a good example of how commercialism can influence popular custom, because even if you choose to ignore the day, you can be made to feel guilty by not keeping up with your peers. Face it—no one wants to be labelled an uncaring boss or an ungrateful staffer.

Like many commercial holidays, this one is American in origin. It was the brainchild of Patricia Bays Haroski, a young secretary from Chicago. In 1958, she received a gift of candy and flowers from her own supervisor at the State Farm Insurance Company in observance of Secretary's Day. She apparently felt an overwhelming urge to reciprocate the gesture, and promptly registered October 16 as National Boss Day with the United States Chamber of Commerce.

She selected October 16 because it was the birthday of her father, a man she said was "an exemplary boss." Unfortunately for Patricia Haroski (and her father), the holiday wasn't a runaway success. In fact, it took so long to catch on that Hallmark, the giant American greeting card company, didn't issue its first Boss's Day card until 1979. But, by the 1990s, the holiday started to take off—at least in the United States. In Nova Scotia I've only seen references to Boss's Day it in the past five years. But, I'll be watching to see where it goes.

John Marshall responding to employees' thanks during Nimbus Publishing's twentieth birthday party.

HALLOWEEN OCTOBER 31

For Wiccans and some other neo-pagans, October 31 is New Year's Eve. However, it is more commonly called Samhain (end of the warm season). Celebrants follow an ancient celebration in acknowledgement of the harvest and the coming of winter. For the ancient Celts, this meant offerings gifts to the gods, which, some historians claim, they got by going from door to door to collect food for the ceremonies and kindling to light the sacred bonfires. The bonfires were there to light the way for the spirits of the dead, who were said to be given free reign on this sacred eve. But, it also meant that evil spirits such as witches, goblins, and bad fairies were free to roam about. At the end of the evening's festivities, the embers from the bonfires were carried home in a hollowed out turnip or gourd to re-light the family's hearth fire. So as not to be confronted by any evil presence that might be about, those carrying the sacred fire back to their homes disguised themselves with masks and strange attire. Over time, and because Samhain activities began to be associated with the rituals of black magic, people confused the two and introduced many of the folk beliefs we now associate with what we call Halloween.

The term "Halloween" originated with the Christian celebration of All Hallow's Eve—the evening before All Saints' Day. "Hallow" is an Old English word for "saint." In many countries, whose primary religion is Catholicism, Halloween is purely a religious celebration. But in Great Britain and North America it is a melding of the ancient Celtic Samhain and All Hallow's Eve. Over time, this phrase was shortened to Hallowe'en and finally to Halloween.

By examining many of the beliefs and rites surrounding Samhain, it is easy to see where many of our own Halloween customs originated. Some of those celebrations came with the early settlers to North America, but it seems that the majority came with the Irish immigrants in the mid-to-latter part of the nineteenth century.

While today's Halloween traditions revolve around trick and treating and dressing in costumes, and feature iconography of witches in pointed hats, black cats, pumpkins, and ghosts, there are some customs that still harken back to the ancient rituals of the Celts. But, for the majority of celebrants, it's a costume party and a chance to get a lot of loot. In fact, more candy is sold at Halloween than any other holiday, and it is second only to Christmas in total retail sales. The cries of "trick or treat" are merely echoes of cash register bells for Halloween merchants.

Over the years Halloween treats have altered drastically. I'm old enough (born in 1950) to remember being on the cusp of treat evolution. I fondly remember getting homemade fudge, candy, and plain apples, Rice Krispies squares wrapped in waxed paper and, even once (by a well-meaning but unthinking soul), homemade frozen fruit-ice on a stick. (I guess she forgot to tell us about it before she tossed it into our pillow cases.) Lucky the youngster who received some of the molasses kisses wrapped in decorative Halloween paper, and a chocolate bar or a bag of potato chips was a real treasure—one to be heralded throughout the neighborhood. In the 1950s, safety was not an issue and children roamed at will in any neighborhood.

That innocence was lost in the late 1960s when some disturbed people began to slip adulterated treats into the loot bags. Although many of the reports of razor blades in apples and LSD in candy have been proven to be urban myths, enough legitimate examples crop up every year to make many parents and guardians forbid their charges to go trick-or-treating. Now, many neighborhoods and communities organize structured, well supervised, Halloween parties.

Another Halloween tradition that has had to struggle through bad press, and later fear tactics, is the collection of coins for the orange and black UNICEF boxes. The "Trick-or-Treat for UNICEF" tradition began in Philadelphia in 1950 when a youth group collected $17 in decorated milk cartons on Halloween to help children overseas. Since then, the United Nations Children's Fund (UNICEF) has distributed millions of boxes to children so they can collect money at Halloween. But that too, suffered from urban myths. During the 1950s, several schools in the United States banned the UNICEF boxes because of rumors that the money collected was used for some communist plot. Today, it is the fear of robbery by other revellers that has forced many children to stop bringing their donation boxes along with them when they go out collecting candy. Maybe the people stealing the boxes are real petty thieves, or maybe they're only fooling around—it's still a pretty mean trick. But that's nothing new. As long as there has been treating—there have been tricks!

One of the more popular folk names for Halloween in Nova Scotia gives a strong clue to the kinds of pranks played by people years ago. Cabbage Night or Cabbage Stump Night was so named because any frost-bitten and rotting cabbages, or the long, gnarled stumps left in the garden after the vegetable had been harvested, were fair game for the tricksters, who would gather these stinking projectiles and throw them on doorsteps or against doors. A strong cabbage stump could also be used as a cudgel. Acadian children around the French Shore would open doors and roll or throw cabbages and other unharvested vegetables into the house.

Helen Creighton collected a song in Gaelic from Angus MacLellan, Grand Mira, Cape Breton, titled, "Creach Na Samhna/The Halloween Raid." Composed somewhere around 1872 or 1873 in Cape Breton by Angus Campbell, who immigrated from Scotland, the long song is about a raid conducted on a cabbage patch on Halloween night. Apparently, the story behind the song is that young people raided the patch, but the bard Campbell made up the song and listed every old man in the area as taking part. The complete version can be found in *Gaelic Songs in Nova*

Scotia by Helen Creighton and Calum MacLeod.

Another popular trick, played out in the days of horses and wagons, was to disassemble a wagon and reassemble it on the roof of the barn—obviously not the work of children there! And, there are hundreds of stories of some poor unsuspecting soul sitting patiently in the outside privy or outhouse finding himself flung "arse-over-tin-kettle" when the entire structure was tipped over or, worse, rolled down an incline. Mind you, you have to ask yourself, given the frequency of this prank, why would anyone use the outhouse on Halloween when a chamber pot would ensure their safety—and dignity? Another trick played before the days of inside plumbing was to holler up the outside sink drain causing the house to be filled with spooky moans and cries. This brought danger to the trickster because the people inside could get their revenge on you with a rush of soapy water. So, the trick could be played from both ends!

Yet another trick from years ago involved making noise makers called "tick-tacks." There were three different models used and I must admit to making and using the last version myself. (Now, I caution you, I give these as examples of material folk culture and not blueprints for the manufacture of Halloween pranks.)

The first model involved an empty wooden sewing thread spool with notches cut around the edges, like the edges of a coin. When a stick was placed through the hole, the spool could be spun against the glass of a house window making a horrible racket inside. The second involves a piece of string

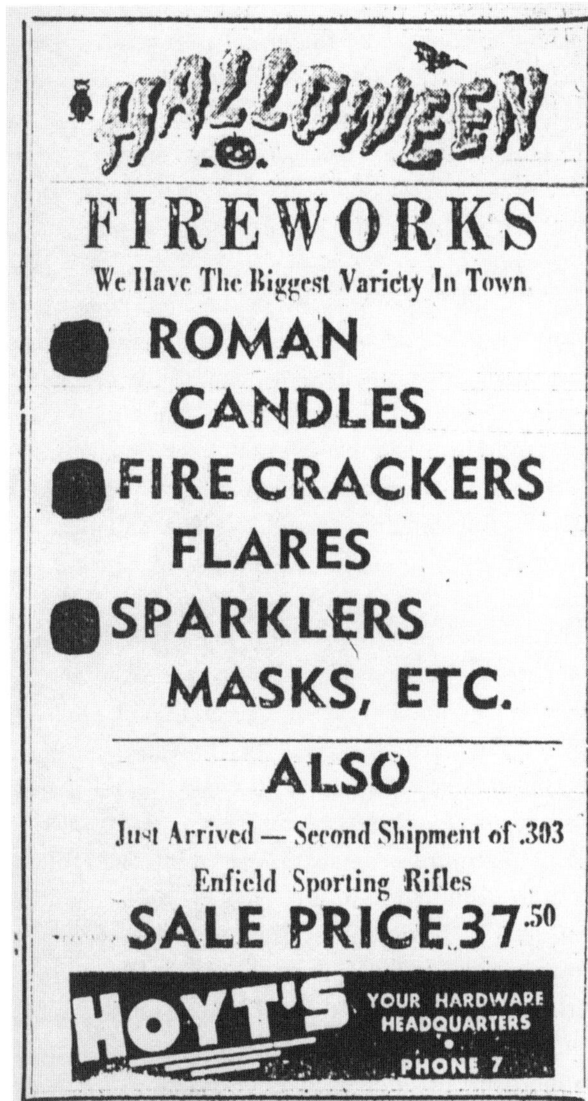

rubbed with rosin stolen from the fiddle case of a local musician. When the taut string was snapped against the window a resounding crack was sure to startle the occupants. The third (and one verified to work by me when I was a teenager) involved less risk of getting caught—a long piece of string or fishing line was tied to a fish hook or safety pin and that was wedged against the window glass. When the string was drawn taut and rubbed with rosin, it could be scraped or plucked causing the metal to squeal against the glass producing the perfect Halloween screams.

Similar toys were made by children in the southern end of the province, only they used buttons or spools attached to string in such as way that they could be rotated on the cord. In her collection of folklore from Shelburne County titled *The Chestnut Pipe*, Marion Robertson refers to these toys as "whiz buttons" and "jinny spinners." Children in Cape Breton made a very different kind of toy called "squibs"—short feather quills packed alternately with dry and damp gunpowder. After being placed on the floor, the squib was lit at the dry end, then fire and sparks spat and shot across the floor until the fire hit some of the damp gunpowder. Then it smoldered for a bit, until the spark touched the dry powder and the squib took off again.

It seems fires and Halloween go together—perhaps a primal throwback to the sacred bonfires in Celtic tradition, except today, its burning tires on the highway or ill-conceived arson involving old or abandoned buildings. One thing is certain—Halloween pranks will always be with us as long as the holiday is seen as a licence to abandon restraint and common sense.

Fortunately, some Halloween customs are harmless, even if they aren't played out as often as they were in former years. The custom of bobbing for apples or trying to bite an apple suspended from a string goes in and out of fashion. In the November 1, 1924 edition of the *Acadian Recorder*, one writer lamented the loss of the apple-bobbing tradition. It hadn't really "passed away altogether." It was a popular Halloween pastime at my house when I was a boy and we even played it when I was a teen at the Presbyterian youth group in Halifax.

Still, other customs have been revived, especially traditional foods once used to celebrate Halloween. In many areas of southwestern Nova Scotia, especially Lunenburg County, a dish of Kolh Cannon (Colcannon) used to be a popular item through the winter months, and had special significance on Halloween. It's made by mashing boiled cabbage, turnips, and potatoes with butter. On Halloween a ring and a thimble were added to the mixture, and whoever got the tokens knew their fate. The ring signified an upcoming marriage; the thimble doomed the finder to a single life. In another version of the recipe, the maker buried a penny, match, ring, and button for marriage, old maid, money, and poverty. Arthur Fauset (who collected primarily among African Nova Scotians) was told of the tradition of putting a gold ring into cooked cabbage—whoever gets it will be the first to marry. Cabbages were also used by the Acadians in making a special soup that was often served on Halloween, but was more often reserved for the next day—All Saints' Day (see November).

Nova Scotians of Scottish heritage frequently turned to a comfort food known as forach (fuarag) which is made by cooking raw oats with thick cream and sugar. Although it was (and often still is) enjoyed any time of the year, it was a traditional dish served on Halloween, both to those at home and to any visitors who might drop by. And, like Kohl Cannon, Halloween forach played a part in divination. A ring was buried in the mush and the first young woman to find it would be the next to get married.

Although we don't see a lot of divination surrounding Halloween customs these days, it was once a very important aspect of the holiday. Arthur Fauset, Helen Creighton, and Marion Robertson all collected interesting examples:

On Halloween take a mirror and walk backwards and look and you will see the face of your future husband. (Creighton)

Unmarried people would attempt to take a bite out of an apple bobbing in a pail of water, or suspended on a string. The first person to do so was believed to be the next to marry. (Creighton)

Go down the cellar backwards with a mirror in your hand and a candle, and your sweetheart will look over your shoulder. (Fauset)

Look in the well and you will see your future husband. (Creighton)

Girls lowered the end of a ball of yarn down the well and walked three times around it chanting an incantation hoping to see their future husbands, and at 12 o'clock midnight they combed their hair before a mirror hoping to see their future husband. (Robertson)

On Halloween night take a human skull and lay it on the ground. Fire a gun at the moon and three drops of blood will drip down and fall into the eye socket of the skull. Put a ball of shot into that socket, put it in a gun and you can fire it at any enemy you like. If the ball doesn't find the enemy, it will come back and go in your own pocket. (Creighton)

Skulls, blood, the forces of darkness—these too are part of the iconography surrounding Halloween. These images associated with death are representations of the spirits rising to life in Celtic lore. The Celts believed that the veil separating the living world from the spirit world was thinnest at Samhain. Spirits could return to earth and take over the bodies of animals—oftentimes a cat. People practising the black arts were said to communicate with these familiars, so the black cat became a symbol of the Halloween spirits visiting on earth.

The other major Halloween symbol is the jack-o'-lantern. Here we find a blending of the ancient pagan vessel used to carry the sacred embers home from the Samhain bonfires, and an Irish folk tale. The Irish tale begins with a man named Jack who had a reputation for being exceedingly mean. One day, he somehow tricked the devil into climbing an apple tree. Once the devil was perched in the branches, Jack cut a crucifix symbol in the bark of the trunk, thus making it impossible for the devil to get down past the holy mark. Years later, when Jack died, he was denied access to heaven because of his meanness and, since the devil remembered his little trick with the apple tree, he was also denied access to hell. He was forced to roam the earth forever. But the devil, apparently recognizing and appreciating a real nasty fellow, offered him one concession. He was given a piece of coal to light his path, which he carried inside a hollowed-out turnip.

It seems that when the early Celtic settlers came to North America, they brought this tale, but substituted the turnip for the pumpkin that was introduced to them by the First Nations peoples. Hollowed out pumpkins became common fare for the early colonists, who made a simplified version of a pumpkin pie by hollowing out the pumpkin and baking it with a filling of apples, molasses, spices, and milk.

So, a hollowed pumpkin would be an obvious choice for a Halloween light. It could hold a candle without fear of catching fire and the rind could be carved and cut to resemble Jack or the devil. In fact, here in Nova Scotia, lighted and hollowed pumpkins were sometimes called pumpkin eaters or pumpkin devils. In Lunenburg County, people who dressed up at Halloween were called jack-o'-lanterns. But, not all jack-o'-lanterns were fashioned from pumpkins. In Shelburne County they were also made from boxes.

Nova Scotia can also lay claim to being the birthplace of the world's largest jack-o'- lantern source, thanks to the efforts of Howard Dill, who began growing giant pumpkins in the 1960s and first became world champion in 1976. He now sends pumpkin seeds all over the world. Imagine the jack-o'-lanterns Howard Dill could carve!

Nova Scotia's early settlers would be amazed at the range of Halloween costumes available today. Years ago, people would dress in old clothes—sometimes wearing clothes of the opposite gender. A cloth case pulled over the head with holes cut for vision might

be the only mask. In the Victorian era, costumes from fancy dress balls might have seen additional use around Halloween, and early in the twentieth century costumes were made at home by clever and imaginative needleworkers. That all changed in the late 1940s when commercial costumes were marketed to post-war children whose parents had some disposable income.

In the 1950s, crepe paper costumes could be bought for less than a dollar. They were great until they got wet—and it almost always seemed to rain on Halloween. By the time the costume-wearers arrived home they'd be lucky if a tiny remnant of stretchy, non-colourfast paper was still hanging on. Now costumes can be rented from specialty houses, patterns can be bought for the home sewers, and a myriad of designs and character outfits can be purchased at the local grocery store. Each year the styles and popular icons change. I began writing this chapter in the year 2002 HP (after Harry Potter) and wizard costumes are all the rage. Next year—who knows? A lot will depend on the current trends.

Even forms of celebrations have come and gone out of fashion. Costume house parties used to be popular in the first half of the twentieth century. Then, with urban development and long rows of houses, kids wanted to be on the streets to gather more goodies. In the 1970s, Halifax was host to a series of very popular Halloween parties erroneously called "Mardi Gras." This night of revels took to the streets in 1983. But, over the years, due to rowdy vandals and lack of support from civic officials, the spontaneous aspect of that celebration is gone. Now people go to professional "haunted houses" and "chambers of horrors."

Halloween, once an evening of harvest celebration and spectral splendor, is turning into another theme night orchestrated by commercialism. But, never fear, as long as humans have an innate fear of the unknown, they will look for ways to celebrate those fears. Halloween has been with us for a long time and, I believe it isn't going anywhere. Like all other aspects of folklore, Halloween changes, but that's what makes it exciting. So, unwrap another molasses candy kiss, light your jack-o'-lantern, and gather the kids around for a few ghost stories. Let's see…it was a dark and stormy night…

NOVEMBER

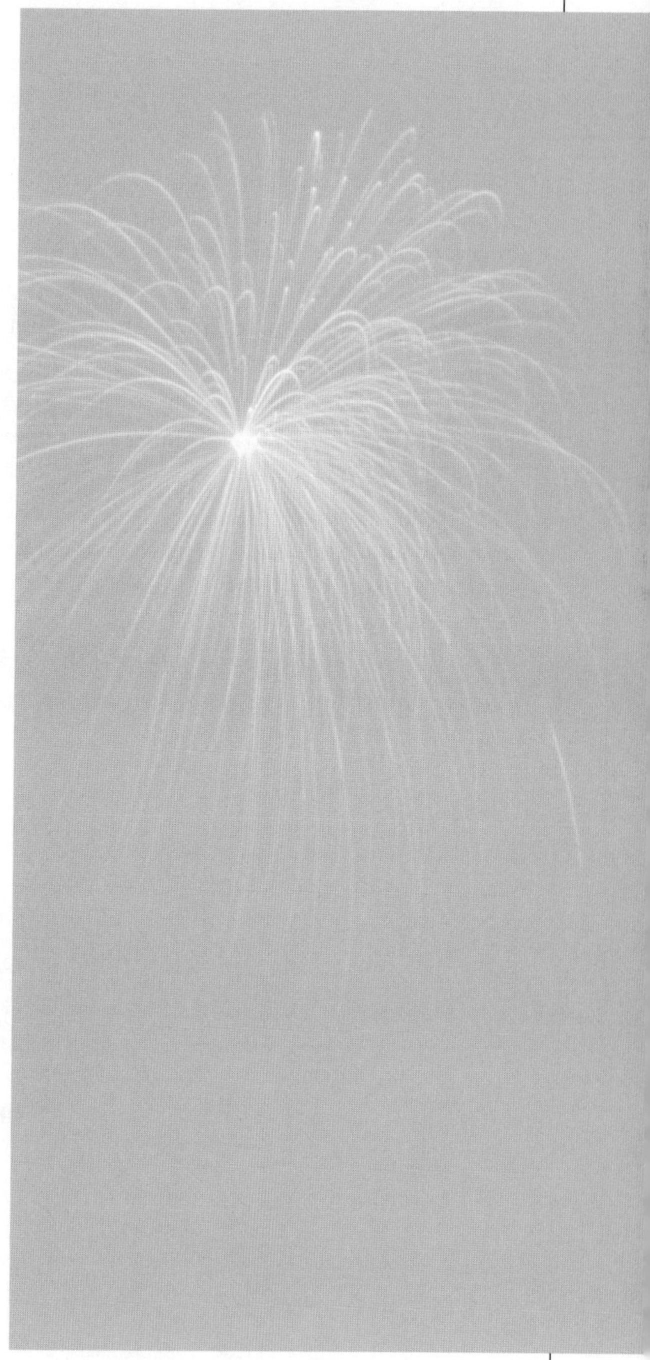

ALL SAINTS' DAY NOVEMBER 1

ALL SAINTS' DAY (All Souls' Day) was created by Pope Boniface IV in the seventh century A.D. to give recognition to all the saints and martyrs who didn't have a special day assigned to them. Originally held on May 13, it was moved by Pope Gregory in the eighth century to the first of November as a counteraction against the pagan celebration of Samhain. The three days from October 31 to November 2 were given the name Hallow Tide.

While this holiday continues to be celebrated primarily within the Catholic religion, not many of the secular customs and traditions associated with it remain active in Nova Scotia. Even in 1928 when Sister Mary Fraser wrote her doctoral thesis, which she later published as *Folklore of Nova Scotia*, the customs associated with All Saints' Day carried on by the elders were already only a memory. A belief she collected in the Antigonish area says: "On this day, the old people used to carry food to their poorer neighbours; careful housewives would never throw water out of doors on All Souls' Night for fear of harming the roaming spirits."

The Acadians know All Saints' Day as a religious holiday called Toussaint. It is traditional to serve *soupe au chou* (cabbage soup), sometimes left over from Halloween, and often made with cabbage said to be "acquired" from a garden the night before.

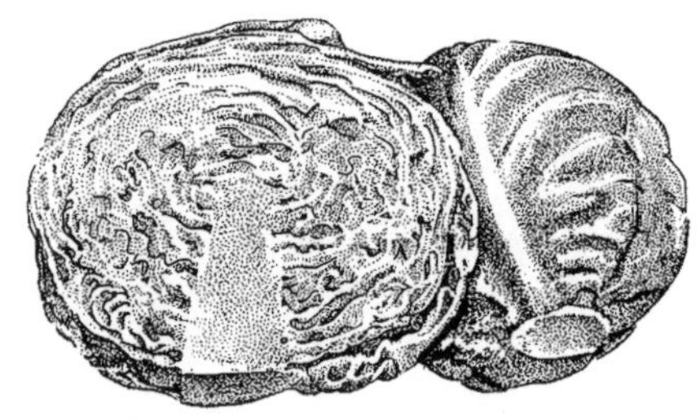

GUY FAWKES DAY NOVEMBER 5

IN BRITAIN, the activities surrounding Guy Fawkes Day, also known as Bonfire Night, include aspects from Samhain mixed with celebrations of a political event that happened in 1605. In that year, a band of Catholic supporters, led by Guy Fawkes, attempted to blow up the House of Commons in London. The plot was discovered and Guy Fawkes was executed. Each year throughout Britain the failed coup (known as the Gunpowder Plot) is celebrated with fireworks, and effigies of Guy Fawkes and the pope are burned.

For many years, Guy Fawkes Day was used as an anti-Catholic celebration, but over the past century, it seems to have taken on more of a festive air. Still, celebrants in Britain make effigies of Sir Guy or "the Guy" and ask for money with the phrase "a penny for the Guy?" Several communities in Great Britain still burn an effigy of the pope, even if some Catholics see the action as a reminder of a much more violent time. This is a good example of a traditional folk custom being distasteful to one particular segment of the population. In 1999, the secretary for the City of Lewes Bonfire Council told the *Catholic Times* that the local Guy Fawkes Day celebrants were commemorating an historic event and were not trying to show disrespect to Pope John Paul II. He added that many Catholics were participating in the revels.

Although Guy Fawkes Day is still celebrated in parts of Newfoundland, it seems to have all but disappeared in Nova Scotia. From diary entries of merchant, privateer, and public servant Simeon Perkins we know how Guy Fawkes Day was celebrated in Queen's County during the early nineteenth century. On November 5, 1810, Perkins headed his entry "Gunpowder Treason" and wrote: "the Colours are displayed on the fort and vessels etc." But what is most fascinating about his diary entry for the following year is that it clearly shows how Guy Fawkes Day traditions had been revived by the town's youth: "November 5, 1811...the Flag is hoisted at the Fort...the Boys carry the pope in the Evening which has not been done here for many years past." Marion Robertson's collection of folklore from Shelburne County provides more detail on this practice. She explains that people would build a bonfire and make a straw or mud effigy of the pope, which they would throw on the fire. People then danced around it, and sometimes boys jumped over it.

When Arthur Fauset was collecting folklore in Nova Scotia in the 1920s, he found some examples of Guy Fawkes Day activities in a celebration called "Pope Day." An image of the pope was dressed in old clothes and a rope was tied around its neck, then it was covered in grease to make it burn easier. Other times the effigy was made from an old tree with added brush and other combustibles. Bonfires were lighted and boys would jump over the flames singing:

Around the Pope,
About the Pope,
Give the Pope a poke (or cut).
Hand me a penny,
To buy some rope,
To hand the butcher (priest)
And burn the Pope.

REMEMBRANCE DAY NOVEMBER 11

In 1918, on the eleventh hour (11:00 a.m.) of the eleventh day of the eleventh month, an armistice was signed at Compiègne in France, ending what the world knew as the Great War and what it hoped would be the war to end all wars. Sadly, that was not the case. The Great War became known as World War One and a succession of conflicts followed it into the twenty-first century. But each November we pause to remember those who serve and those who have fallen. It is an act of remembrance, not celebration. And for many, it is one of our most important holidays.

Remembrance Day was first made a legal holiday in Canada in 1921 when the federal government proclaimed:

> *"Throughout Canada in each week in which the eleventh of November shall occur, being the day in the year one thousand nine hundred and eighteen on which the Great War was triumphantly concluded by an armistice shall be a legal holiday and shall be kept and observed as such under the name of Armistice Day."*

As already mentioned, from 1921 to 1930 Thanksgiving Day and Armistice Day were celebrated together, fixed by statute on the Monday of the week in which the eleventh of November fell. Gradually, a change was brought about, partially out of the desire to hold Armistice celebrations on the actual anniversary of the signing, as was being done in other parts of the Commonwealth. In fact, the *Acadian Recorder* for November 8, 1924, carried the following announcement: "In accordance with arrangements for the observance of Armistice Day, the people of Canada are invited to mark the occasion by a two minute's silence at eleven o'clock am on Tuesday. This is a special observance, suggested by the King, and is in addition to the regular celebration of the date recognized by the Canadian Parliament for Monday."

By 1931, Parliament had adopted an act to amend the Armistice Day Act, declaring that the day should always be observed on November 11 and called Remembrance Day. Since then, each November 11 has been a time for veterans and citizens to gather at cenotaphs and lay wreaths in honour of those who gave "the supreme sacrifice."

When I recall Remembrance Days from my boyhood, especially in Sherbrooke, I liken them to Sundays—no running around and raucous playing in the morning. But what is still most vivid in my mind is the mixture of pride and sadness of my Grandfather MacKay. He wore his medals with honour but always reminded us that it was those comrades he left on the battlefield that deserved the greatest recognition. The day was a time to reminisce, not boast. I'd hear stories of my Grandfather Croft being cut down by machine gun fire, only to be rescued and carried back to safety by his cousin. It was a sacred day—holiday hardly seems the appropriate word.

Today, Remembrance Day is a statutory holiday for government workers and bank employees only. Many businesses close for the morning but reopen after noon.

NOVEMBER 11

Remembrance Day, Halifax 1928, before Boer War Statue at Province House.

If we look back to some earlier Armistice Day celebrations we see that it wasn't all solemn parades and ceremonies at cenotaphs. In the *Acadian Recorder* for November 8, 1924, we read that several dances were planned throughout the city and ladies were advised that they could get new frocks for the Armistice Ball at Mahons in Halifax. Other activities included a "Monster Musical Revue at St Patrick's Hall" called "Frills and Frolics," a revue of songs, dancing, minstrel parts, featuring a new addition to Armistice Day celebrations: "A novelty attraction will be the Armistice poppy, which will be sold during the evening and as each poppy will be numbered all purchasers will have a chance to win $5 in gold."

The poppy has long been used as a memorial symbol for fallen soldiers. Legend says that in Holland after the battle of Neerwinden in 1693, the fields became covered with poppies. The belief was that they grew from the blood of 20,000 men, and was a sign that heaven was angry because of mankind's evil deeds.

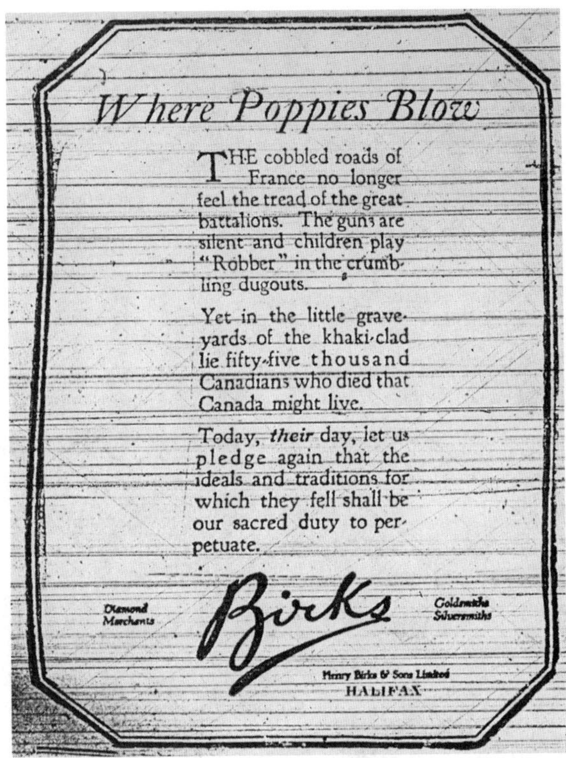

Where Poppies Blow

THE cobbled roads of France no longer feel the tread of the great battalions. The guns are silent and children play "Robber" in the crumbling dugouts.

Yet in the little graveyards of the khaki-clad lie fifty-five thousand Canadians who died that Canada might live.

Today, *their* day, let us pledge again that the ideals and traditions for which they fell shall be our sacred duty to perpetuate.

Diamond Merchants

Birks

Goldsmiths Silversmiths

Henry Birks & Sons Limited
HALIFAX

Years later, in Belgium, the symbol of the poppy was to become an important Canadian legacy in the remembrance of fallen soldiers. Lieutenant-Colonel John McCrae, who was born in Guelph, Ontario, was a medical doctor who served in the Canadian Corp in World War One. In the early morning of May 3, 1915, during the second battle of Ypres, he tore a sheet of paper from his dispatch book and, in twenty minutes, wrote the poem "In Flanders Fields." The British magazine *Punch* published it anonymously in 1915. Doctor McCrae was killed in France in 1918.

In North America the idea of wearing poppies to honour the dead came about for the first time from a young New York City servicemen's canteen worker in 1918. It became an international symbol when, later that same year, a French woman, Madame Guerin, borrowed the idea to use the poppy as a form of fundraising to aid war-torn France. The Flanders poppy was adopted by the British Empire Services League, and in Canada by the Great War Veterans

Armistice Day Parade along Barrington Street, November 11, 1918.

Association, the predecessor of the Royal Canadian Legion, which was established in 1926. The Legion's "Articles of Faith" state that the poppy is the "emblem of supreme sacrifice."

Whenever veterans get together, it's a sure bet that some of the old songs popular during their war will be sung. A Nova Scotian is said to have written one of the most popular and enduring songs from World War One:

Oh, mademoiselle from Armentières, parlez-vous,
Oh, mademoiselle from Armentières, parlez-vous,
Mademoiselle from Armentières,
She hasn't been kissed in forty years, hinky-dinky,
par-lee-voo.

The song is attributed to Lieutenant Gitz Rice, who was born in New Glasgow in 1891. He studied at the McGill Conservatory, and subsequently joined the army's First Canadian Contingent as a gunnery officer. During the war, he was posted to active service in Europe, where he fought in several battles, including those at Ypres, the Somme, and Vimy Ridge. He also helped organize and performed in stage shows to entertain the soldiers on the front lines. One of those places was Armentières, a town in northern France, in Flanders. During most of World War One the town was directly behind the Allied lines. Popular folk history says Lieutenant Rice sat down at a little café in Armentières in 1915, and while observing a chic barmaid serve drinks, he composed the words and adapted the melody from an old tune. He performed his composition a few days later before the Fifth Battery, Montreal, stationed in France. It was an instant hit! After the war, Gitz Rice worked as a professional musician and songwriter. He became known for hit songs such as "Dear Old Pal of Mine," in which a soldier laments his girlfriend's absence. The song was made popular by John McCormack, who adopted it as his signature tune.

During World War Two, Mr. Rice again travelled to the front to entertain Canadian soldiers. He died in New York in October 1947 at the age of 56, but his song lives on in many versions—both clean and bawdy!

World War Two brought a new list of war classics. "I'll Be Seeing You," "The White Cliffs Of Dover" and, in Nova Scotia, the Don Messer show closer "Til We Meet Again" were hugely popular songs that can still be heard in senior's homes and at Legion halls around the province. Nova Scotia's Wilf Carter, known in Canada as "The Grandfather of Country and Western Music," penned a sad song of lovers parted because of the war titled "Put Me In Your Pocket." It was a popular song with my parents when my dad was serving in the army and I remember learning it during drives back and forth from Halifax to Sherbrooke. When I sing it in concert today, the people who knew it during the war sing along and their eyes drift away to another time.

Music, especially the songs we knew during times of strife, can do that. It helps us remember and appreciate the sacrifices made—even if we didn't live through it. And that's what Remembrance Day is all about: remembering. Hopefully one day we can bring reality to the lines of the song penned by my friend, the famed folk singer and composer Ed McCurdy, who made Nova Scotia his home during the last two decades of his life:

Last night I had the strangest dream,
I'd ever dreamed before,
I dreamed the world had all agreed
To put an end to war.

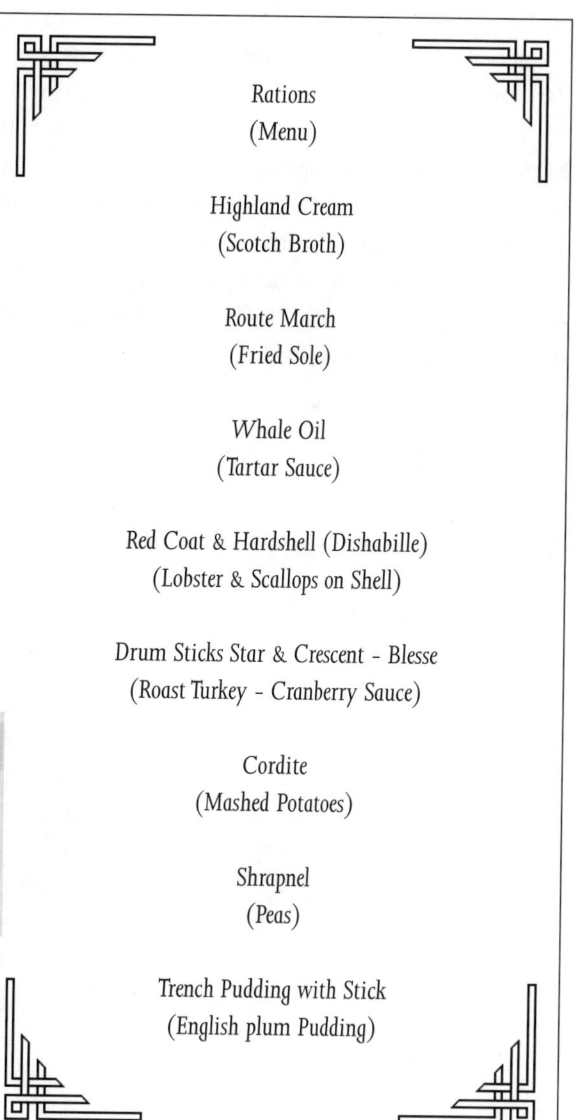
Rations
(Menu)

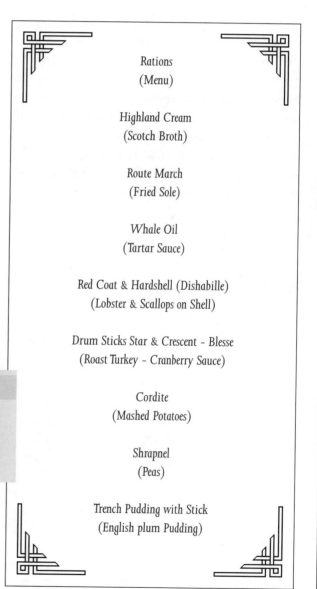

Highland Cream
(Scotch Broth)

Route March
(Fried Sole)

Whale Oil
(Tartar Sauce)

Red Coat & Hardshell (Dishabille)
(Lobster & Scallops on Shell)

Drum Sticks Star & Crescent - Blesse
(Roast Turkey - Cranberry Sauce)

Cordite
(Mashed Potatoes)

Shrapnel
(Peas)

Trench Pudding with Stick
(English plum Pudding)

Menu for an Armistice Dinner held at the Halifax Hotel, November 11, 1926.

ST. ANDREW'S DAY — NOVEMBER 30

ST. ANDREW IS THE PATRON SAINT of Scotland, and his day is celebrated by Scots around the world on November 30. One of Christ's twelve apostles, Andrew is credited with spreading Christianity through Asia Minor and Greece. Legend tells of his crucifixion by the Romans in Patras, southern Greece, by being nailed to a diagonally shaped cross. This X shape is the origin of the cross of St. Andrew, which appears on the Scottish flag. There is also the "Order of St. Andrew" or the "Most Ancient Order of the Thistle"—an ancient order of knighthood that is restricted to the monarch and sixteen others. It was established by James VII of Scotland in 1687.

As we have seen in the entries for *Belcher's Almanac*, published in Halifax for 1870, St. Andrew's Day was once part of the regular holiday roster for the general citizenry in Nova Scotia, but today it is primarily a celebration for those wishing to honour their Scottish heritage.

DECEMBER

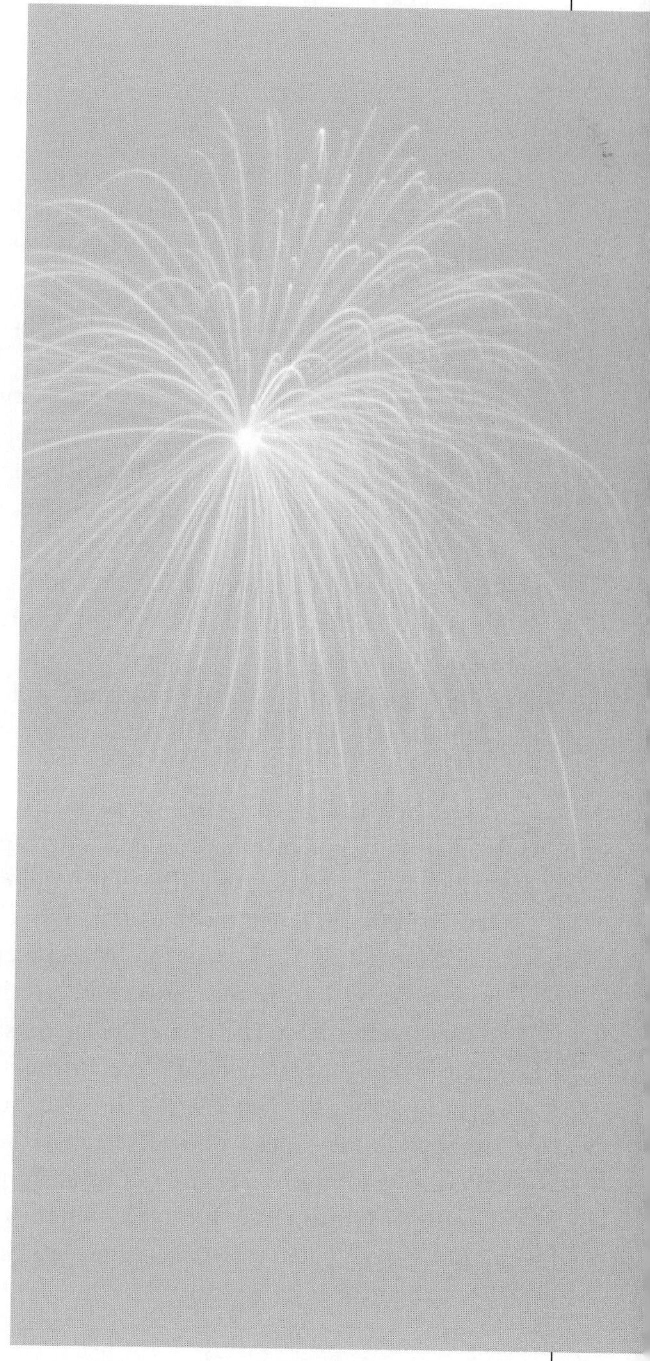

CHRISTMAS DECEMBER 25

CHRISTMAS! There are more examples of music, traditional food, customs and traditions, forms of decorations and iconography, superstitions and beliefs, and commercial attachments associated with the holiday commemorating the birth of Jesus Christ than any other in western society.

The etymology for the word Christmas is late Old English—Cristes Maesse, the Mass of Christ, and was first found in use around 1038 A.D. Around 1131 A.D., it was altered to Cristes-messe. Another common variant of the word is Xmas. Some people think this is a vulgar term for the holiday, but, in fact, it is derived from the Greek letter X ("chi"), the first letter of Christos (Christ). The word Xmas has been in use since the early days of Christianity. In Latin it is known as *Dies Natalis*, which is the origin of the French "*noël*."

In Christian belief, Jesus Christ was born in Bethlehem approximately two thousand years ago. But official recognition of Christ's birth didn't take place within the celebrations of the early church until almost 137 A.D., when the bishop of Rome ordered the birthday of the Christ child be celebrated as a solemn feast. The first evidence outside of Rome of a feast day to honour Christ is from Coptic Egypt in about 200 A.D. Then in 350 A.D. another bishop of Rome, Julius I, chose December 25 as the official date for the observance of Christ's birth. But it wasn't until the fourth century when we saw almost every Western calendar assign Jesus's birth date to December 25.

Even then, Christmas was more of a religious holiday, with New Year's assuming the bulk of secular festivities. But, by the fifteenth century, it had developed into a special time for eating, drinking and making merry!

In England, during the Puritan Reformation, the secular celebration of Christmas was forbidden by an Act of Parliament in 1644. The government decreed that, although the day was to be honoured with fasting, it was to remain a regular market day and merchants were obligated to keep their shops open. After the Restoration, many dissenters still referred to the public celebrations surrounding Christmas as "Fooltide."

Christmas is foremost a Christian religious holiday. In fact, many people who decry the commercialism of the celebrations admonish society to "put Christ back into Christmas." And, although some religious scholars deny any similarity between Christmas traditions and earlier pagan rites, the majority of folk scholars and anthropologists have identified many aspects of Christmas traditions that can be traced back to earlier cultures. Similar traditions can be found in the ancient Mesopotamian celebration of the new year. The Roman festival of Saturnalia (Saturn) was held in what we have come to call December, and the Persians, whose religion Mithraism was one of Christianity's main contemporary rivals, also held that part of the year sacred. I noted earlier that the early Christian hierarchy appropriated many pagan holidays into the rites and celebrations of the Christian church. And hundreds of customs and celebrations have evolved that have no reference to the religious nature of Christmas.

Sacred or secular, Christmas traditions and beliefs continue to be an important part of our modern society. Even non-Christians have to be influenced and affected by Christmas celebrations. In Nova Scotia (as in all of the Western world) many government holidays, retail merchandising, and a plethora of social affairs are geared to the celebration of Christmas. And, while volumes could be (and have been) written on Christmas origins and traditions, I'd like to concentrate on how those traditions evolved in Nova Scotia.

Our earlier ancestors didn't always celebrate in a grand style with an elaborate Christmas dinner. At times, they barely acknowledged the day. From the diary of Simeon Perkins, Liverpool 1773: "Saturday, December 25, Christmas day. I work in the woods. No fresh provisions, so I dine on salt fish." Seven years later, in 1800, Lieutenant Governor Henry Bowyer, issued the following Christmas Day order to his troops: "Christmas is to be observed as Sunday in every respect…except the men be allowed a holiday from 2 o'clock in the afternoon, on condition of their taking no time for dinner." The next year, James Rainstrope Morris, first superintendent of Sable Island, made the following entry in his journal:

Halifax, Xmas, c.1958.
L.to R. back row: Clarence, Carol, Olive;
front: Clary and Nancy Croft.

> "December 25th, 1801: *A Cold frosty Morn—Wind NW: but a merry day, and Hallelujahs should be sung—we saluted this day with a discharge of the Cannon—had an excellent dinner with wild ducks etc—and all tranquil—Day ends stormy & heavy gusts of wind.*"

A Spartan, yet happy Christmas no doubt, but by the mid-Victorian era, Christmas celebrations and the accompanying foods had become far more lavish. The December 19, 1873, edition of the Amherst Gazette posted a notice of a "Concert, Christmas Tree, Grand Supper & Refreshments." It wrote how members of the Acacia Lodge arranged a bazaar at the Masons' Hall in Amherst which featured "a promenade concert by amateur performers and a splendid hot supper."

In the next decade, the Halifax *Morning Chronicle*, December 24, 1888, was able to advertise shipments of "just landed Jamaica oranges, lemons, layered dates, English chestnuts, raisins, clear toys and Rowntree and Company's celebrated chocolates in fancy boxes." Earlier in the month, the same newspaper announced in its December 5 edition: "A game of cricket will be played on Chain Lake, weather permitting," and added, "the usual plum dinner will be given the inmates of the poor asylum." A similar plum dinner was also offered to the inmates of Rockhead Prison in the city's north end.

NORTH SYDNEY FROM THE HARBOR

Vooght Bros. NORTH SYDNEY

The Largest Departmental Store in Lower Provinces.

Full supply of all kinds of Goods always on hand.
Prompt attention given to Mail Orders.........
Carloads of Goods arriving daily..............

Wholesale & Retail

D. G. KIRK. W. E. WHITMAN.

KIRK & WHITMAN,

DIRECT IMPORTERS AND DEALERS IN

Dry Goods, Gents' Furnishings,
Ready-made Clothing, Boots, Shoes,
Granite and Tinware.

ALSO A FULL LINE OF XMAS. NOVELTIES.

Choice Groceries, Home and Foreign FRUITS at ground-floor prices at McLEOD'S, NEAR POST OFFICE. North Sydney.

Merry Christmas.

COME AND SEE OUR TEMPTING DISPLAY.

We have four tons of POULTRY. Special Xmas. BEEF in abundance. Largest, cleanest and best stock of goods for the inner man

PHONE 18. JACKSON & CO., NORTH SYDNEY.

BIG SEASON'S TRADE

Yet have had time to make ample provision for Xmas. needs of our patrons, and have laid in liberal stock of useful articles, such as: Carvers, Skates, Carpet Sweepers, Scissors in cases, Boys' and Girls' Sleighs, etc., etc., etc.

Call at one or other of our stores North Sydney, Glace Bay, Sydney Mines.

The A. C. THOMPSON CO., Ltd.

Puddings boiled in cloth or steamed in moulds were considered the pinnacle of Victorian Christmas desserts. Despite its name, the old fashioned plum pudding had no plums. (The word plum referred to any dried fruits, especially raisins and currants.) An old custom states that each family member must stir the pudding while it is being made. It must be stirred from east to west, in the direction travelled by the Magi. This custom comes from "Stir-up" Sunday, which occurs about five weeks before Christmas and derives from the Church of England's Common Book of Prayer for that Sunday: "Stir up, We beseech Thee, O Lord, the wills of Thy faithful people."

Plum puddings were sometimes referred to as mince (or mincemeat) puddings. Mincemeat is also a traditional filling for pies. In the seventeenth century, mincemeat was the "meat" of dried fruits and nuts, baked in rectangular pies to represent the Christ child's manger. They were pungent with spices, thought to represent the exotic gifts brought by the Magi. During the Reformation in England, the Puritans, objecting to the religious associations with a common food, outlawed the serving of these pies. They are now made with dried fruits and nuts and many people add ground beef or pork. Others maintain that venison makes the best pies, while in Cape Breton, a popular meatless variant is called pork pie.

Several other traditional desserts in Nova Scotia are often regional or cultural specialties. Fruitcakes are very popular and many families have recipes that have been handed down for generations. If the tradition in the family leaned toward temperance, the baked cake, laden with dried and candied fruits and nuts, might be served in its unadorned form, with perhaps the addition of some marzipan or sugar icing. If, however, the odd drop of black rum or brandy was kept in the house, the cake could be soaked in this elixir for months before the Christmas holiday season. I well imagine many a temperance "blue ribbon" wearer broke the pledge with a slice or two of Christmas cake. Besides, you couldn't risk insulting your host or risking bad luck. One popular belief found throughout the province said that between Christmas and Epiphany, you must accept Christmas cake at every house you visit. In Bridgewater, this delicacy was often called suet cake. By whatever name it was called, the belief was that each piece of cake eaten would bring a month of happiness for the coming year.

Even Victorian-era children got in on the illicit fun of enjoying spirits. A popular game for children was "snapdragon." in which raisins were soaked in brandy, then ignited, while the children would grab for the flaming fruits. If they were slow, they got burned raisins with the alcohol burned off. But if they were good at the game, they got hot raisins and the chance of getting a Christmas buzz.

Acadian children were given "naulets"—cookies made with sugar and molasses and shaped to resemble the Christ child. They were sometimes called *catins au sucre* (sugar dolls) or *catins au mélasse* (molasses dolls). *Beignes à la mélasse* (molasses doughnuts) were another kind of Acadian Christmas treat.

During the Middle Ages a bread called "Bretzel" was made to celebrate the winter solstice. Circular with an extra twist of dough on top, which formed a cross representing the four seasons, the bread was adopted by Christians, who said the shape symbolized praying hands. In Lunenburg, a variant of this bread can still be found today and is most commonly called a pretzel.

In Shelburne County, a popular form of Christmas sugar cookies are called "santys." They were often

Christmas dinner with troops and members of the Salvation Army, Red Shield Hostel, Halifax, 1941.

made to give to the people who came door to door in a tradition similar to mumming. (See belsnickling.)

Today, the mainstay of the modern Christmas dinner is the turkey, but this wasn't always the featured item on the Christmas dinner menu. In the nineteenth century, turkeys were considered such a costly novelty that entrepreneurs set up turkey shoots where one bought tickets for the opportunity to bag a turkey. To ensure a successful "shoot," the birds would be buried up to their necks in snow. The marksman's meal might have been enjoyed with the tart accompaniment of cranberries picked by hand or brought in huge barrels from Sable Island.

For most Nova Scotians, geese, domestic ducks, and wild birds were the holiday fowl of choice, but in Lunenburg County, a popular meal at Christmas was salt ribs and sauerkraut. Other common Christmas fare included eels, rabbits, and porcupine stuffed as one would a chicken. Porcupine could have been one type of wild game found in a Chezzetcook Acadian meat pie called "garteau," which was traditionally served after mass on Christmas Eve, the main time for the Christmas celebratory meal. Other Acadian dishes popular throughout the year, but given special care at Christmas, include *poutine râpé* (made with grated potatoes, cheese, and some form of meat or fish, including quahogs and clams), *fricot au lièvre* (rabbit stew), *pâté à la ràpure* (rappie pie, whose base ingredient is grated potatoes with the starch removed), *boudin du pays* (blood pudding, usually made during Lent but often saved for Christmas), and savory meat pies with pastry crusts called *tourtières*. Since I married into an Acadian family over thirty years ago, *tourtière* with yellow chow has become a traditional Christmas Eve treat.

Another Acadian food tradition found especially in the southwestern end of the province (known as the Pubnicos) is a Christmas biscuit containing two beans or two pennies. The first two people to find them would be crowned *le roi et la reine*—the king and queen.

Everyone has their own comfort foods at Christmas—foods that evoke memories of childhood. I never liked the sweet, brightly coloured syrup that we used to mix with water and have at the "children's table" for Christmas dinner. But all I have to do is open a bottle and smell the concentrate and I am transported back to the age of seven and Christmas dinner in my grandparents' dining room in the "big house" in Sherbrooke.

Few people in other parts of Canada can understand why Nova Scotians like to have at least a few cinnamon and chocolate flavored candies called "chickenbones" at Christmas. And even though the brand has been taken over by an American chocolate giant, a box of Pot of Gold chocolates still evokes the time when the Moir's chocolate factory reigned supreme in Halifax. After all, we all knew that Pot of Gold was Santa's choice for the chocolates he put in our stockings.

The origins of Santa Claus—that jolly old Christmas elf—are varied. His most distinct characteristics can be traced back to a fourth-century Turkish bishop named Nicholas who had a reputation for being both kind and generous. Many folk tales of his largess have been collected, with the most common motifs having him drop money down a chimney to help a maiden (or maidens) in need. The money lands in stockings hung before the fire.

Nicholas became the patron saint of children, orphans, sailors, and even thieves, as well as of Russia and Greece. His feast day was held on the anniversary of his death, December 6. On the eve of this feast, children would put out treats for him and his horse as he made his rounds delivering small tokens to the good children and sticks to the bad. The legend of Nicholas spread and he became known in several forms throughout Europe and parts of Asia Minor. In Germany, he was called *Weihnachtsmann*, in France, *Père Noël*, and in England, Father Christmas.

In the 1600s, Dutch colonists brought the *Sinterklaas* (Saint Nicholas) traditions to North America. Over time his name was altered to sound more like Santy Claus and eventually Santa Claus. In 1808, American author Washington Irving helped in establishing the image of the colonial Santa Claus in his satirical work "Diedrich Knickerbocker's History of New York from the Beginning of the World to the End of the Dutch Dynasty." His description of a jolly Dutchman who smoked a long-stemmed clay pipe and wore baggy breeches and a broad-rimmed hat stuck. Then, in 1822, Dr. Clement Clarke Moore published his famous poem "A Visit from St. Nicholas," better known as "The Night Before Christmas." His description of the elf who delivered toys with the help of Arctic reindeer not only gave Santa Claus a home in the north but a physical description that he maintains: "He had a broad face, and a little round belly, that shook, when he laughed, like a bowl full of jelly." His appearance was further embellished with the 1863 illustration of "A Visit from St. Nicholas" by German immigrant Thomas Nast. It was with these illustrations that we see Santa dressed in red clothing with fur trim. For the next twenty-three years, Thomas Nast's illustrations of Santa Claus appeared in the American magazine *Harper's Weekly*, helping to codify his image well into the 1900s. In 1931, artist Haddon Sundblom began creating a Santa image for the *Coca-Cola* company that has become the quintessential jolly, twinkly-eyed character we know today.

My first memories of Santa Claus are of sitting on his knee at Sunday school in the basement of the Presbyterian church in Sherbrooke. Later, when we moved to Halifax, I discovered he also went to the department stores. It didn't take long for me to realize that Santa had many "helpers," some of whom had better outfits than others. At the annual family Christmas parties held by the Princess Louise Fusiliers at the Halifax armories (my dad was in the reserve army there), I was intrigued to find that Santa smelled of Old Spice aftershave and Captain Morgan rum. I knew he wasn't the real Santa, but went along with the ruse because he gave out such neat gifts. Besides, I was certain I had the goods on the real Santa. I first heard his voice on CHNS Radio and later saw him on television. He was the real thing—dressed just right, with a voice that was full of authority and sweetness. When

Santa and two elf children with
a Moir's chocolate advertisement, c.1950.

I grew up and started to work on television myself, I got to know the man who "helped" Santa. His name was Bill Fulton and, like Santa, he was a kind, jolly soul. All I had to do was hear his voice and I was instantly transported back to my childhood, listening to the radio and reciting the Christmas pledge:

> *I promise to be good in every way, so that I can help make every day, almost as happy as Christmas Day.*

An important nineteenth-century addition to the Santa Claus lore is the presence of reindeer. This association between the Christmas elf and members of the caribou family may be traced back to the Norse god Odin, who travelled with his reindeer delivering gifts of grain and fruit to the children. We find the first reference to Santa using reindeer in an 1821 poem titled "Santeclaus," by William Galley, which describes the old gent dressed in fur and driving a sleigh pulled by one reindeer. The next year, Clement Moore added seven more celestial steeds to the roster, even naming the individual deer in "A Visit from St. Nicholas." But we had to wait more than 125 years to meet "the most famous reindeer of all."

The American retailer The Montgomery Ward Company had for years been buying and giving out colouring books for Christmas at their stores. One of their employees, copywriter Robert May, wrote a story about a little reindeer with extraordinary powers. Denver Gillen from the "Monkey Ward's" art department illustrated it. The company executives liked the innocent tale, and in 1939 they had almost 2.5 million booklets printed and distributed. Songwriter Johnny Marks wrote a musical version of the story and, in 1949, cowboy singer Gene Autry recorded his biggest hit "Rudolph the Red-nosed Reindeer."

Over the years many different methods of communicating with Santa have been employed. The *South Shore Record* (Mahone Bay) for December 16, 1937, carried the following announcement: "Another feature, particularly popular with the kiddies, is the sending of Santagrams. These are telegrams dated from the North Pole."

Today, children can send regular and electronic messages to the North Pole or they can visit one of the thousands of Santa's helpers stationed in brightly-coloured chairs at the shopping malls. A more traditional method used in Nova Scotia to communicate with Santa was to write him a note then burn it in the stove or chimney. Santa could read your message in the smoke that rose above your house. If the letter-writer wanted some doll clothes, threads were burned along with the letter. Once the message was delivered, all one had to do was wait and hope.

Then, in a custom harkening back to the legends of Saint Nicholas and the maidens receiving gifts in their stockings hung on the fireplace, our own stockings were laid out to receive the largess. Today, many children and adults have special Christmas stockings, lavishly decorated and monogrammed. When my parents were children, they put out heavy hand-knit wool socks. I, like many young boys in 1950s Nova Scotia, wore much-hated long brown stockings exactly like those of my older sister Carol. The only decent concession to having to sport these things was that they could hold a lot of Christmas goodies. And, although nailing stockings to the mantelpiece seemed to be the custom for most of the children I knew, we never hung our stockings on the fireplace, even when we had one. We always laid or tied our stocking on our bed. In areas of Nova Scotia with a strong German heritage, children didn't hang stockings at all. At Riverport they put out shoes; at Ironbound they put out plates with a gift of food for Santa, expecting them to be graced with gifts in return.

Depending on the circumstances of one's family, Christmas gifts could be simple and homemade or lavish and store-bought. There was a time when people referred to Christmas gift "giving" as opposed to Christmas "shopping." That's because they made most of the gifts they gave. Years ago, almost all Christmas gifts were homemade, and in many households, the only gifts you received were those that came in a stocking.

In the Victorian era these gifts could include raisins, figs, nuts, an orange in the toe, and sometimes a piece of coal or potato as a friendly reminder of the past year's sins. A child was fortunate to receive one small store-bought toy. When parents could afford luxuries, additional treats might be small toys, puzzles, books, and maybe a piece or two of the delicious rock-hard barley toys from the Yarmouth Candy

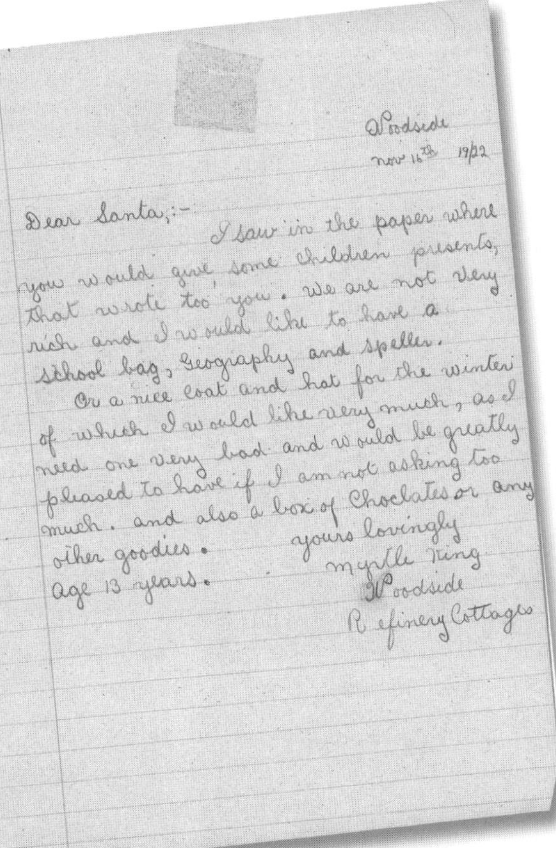

Woodside
nov 16th 19/22

Dear Santa;:-
I saw in the paper where
you would give some children presents,
that wrote too you. We are not very
rich and I would like to have a
school bag, Geography and speller.
Or a nice coat and hat for the winter
of which I would like very much, as I
need one very bad and would be greatly
pleased to have if I am not asking too
much. and also a box of Choclates or any
other goodies. yours lovingly
Age 13 years. Myrtle King
Woodside
Refinery Cottages

This poignant letter was written in response to a contest in the Halifax *Morning Chronicle*, 1922.

Company, which began manufacturing these Christmas candies in the 1800s.

Handkerchiefs were always popular with girls. A common saying was the number of handkerchiefs received at Christmas, the number of years before the girl married. Homemade handkerchiefs were frequently embroidered with an innocent romantic saying or a verse from the Bible. Religious toys were popular, at least with the parents. Often called "Sunday toys," because they were the only playthings allowed on the Sabbath, these included puzzles featuring scenes of biblical events and carved wooden Noah's Arks.

Soldiers and military toys were popular for boys, while dolls and doll clothes were popular for girls. During the nineteenth century, Christmas church bazaars were extremely popular and often people could buy a complete travelling wardrobe, including little trunks, for the child's doll.

In sea-faring families, it was common for the boys to receive a beautiful hand-carved and fully-rigged sailing boat, often a replica of a ship sailed in by a family member. In the early nineteenth century, Joseph Connally, a lighthouse keeper on the Bay of Fundy, wrote in his dairy: "sat up last night and whittled a wheelbarrow from driftwood as a Christmas present for my small son."

Gift making and giving was not exclusively saved for children. Most nineteenth-century children were expected to make some sort of Christmas gift for the adults in their family. It was not only a way to show off their skills, but a lesson in the adage "it is better to

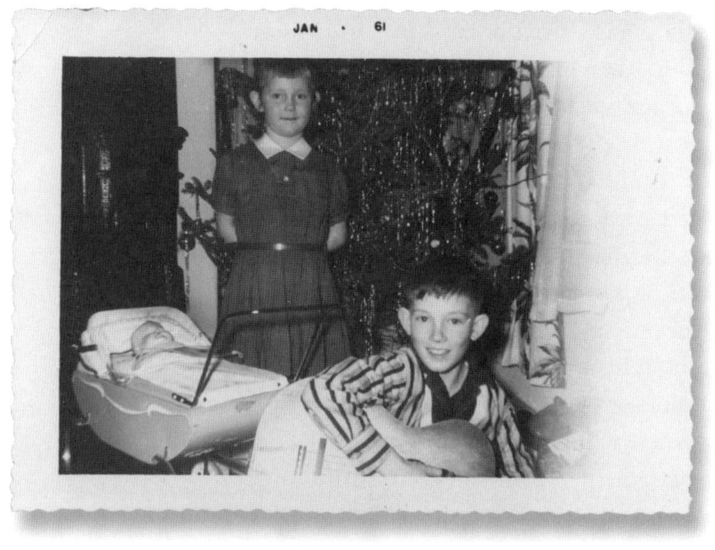

Xmas, Halifax, 1960. Nancy and Clary Croft.

"I was ten and this was my first guitar."

give than to receive!" Young girls embroidered slippers and pen wipes; boys carved letter openers and door stops.

Children made tableaus, sometimes with shadow figures, of Bible scenes or historical events, especially for their parents. Nativity scenes were particularly appreciated. It was also popular to send a lock of one's hair in the Christmas letter to perhaps be made into a friendship or family wreath of human hair flowers.

When adults exchanged gifts, they were frequently simple expressions of their skill in homemaking or hunting. Bottles of homemade blueberry wine or blackberry cordial, which would be just about ripe by Christmas time, were always welcomed, except perhaps in a home where temperance was the norm. People who couldn't get their own game would be offered a pair of rabbits for the Christmas Eve pie or a bottle of preserved moose meat.

And, if you had money, the sky was the limit. Ships brought goods from all over the world. From the Halifax *Morning Chronicle*, December 24, 1888: "F. W. Powers, the north end druggist...has a good assortment of Xmas stock and reports trade good. Mr. Powers has a fine lot of cards, perfumes, cigars and pipes...these and numerous other items to kill and cure make the store very attractive."

In the twentieth century, styles of gifts for children and adults not only changed but the number of gifts given has increased. Still, it was often the ones made by hand and with love that were the most cherished. As a girl, my mother received a doll's furniture set, with cradle and tiny rocking chair, hand-carved by her grandfather Burns and painted with boat paint. It is as treasured today as it was then.

One of the most dramatic changes to take place in gift giving came about with the rise in popularity of mail-order catalogues. Although they were common by the turn of the century, it wasn't until after the Depression that people began making substantial Christmas orders from the "Wish Book." In rural areas, it brought an opportunity to see goods one could only dream of and put many shoppers on equal footing with their neighbors. All you needed was the money! And, if you didn't have the cash, generous credit terms were available. You could buy in December and have it paid off by the end of the following November, just in time to send in your Christmas order again.

It might be said that mail-order catalogues, and the proliferation of commercial gifts available to the masses, put an end to most of the handmade and crafted gifts so popular in the previous century. It wasn't until the early 1970s that craft fairs made a boom business out of homemade gifts—only this time they weren't made by the giver. Christmas craft fairs have become so popular in Nova Scotia that the vendors have to start selling their wares in October. And even many of these fairs have moved beyond the simple craft variety of goods to fine art pieces—with prices to match. However, for most children, a handmade gift can't compete with the high-tech toys and gadgets available today.

Dear Clarence: Jan. 1960
Do you know that of all creams for my hands I like Avon Cream the best of all. You couldn't have given me a more acceptable gift. Thank you very much fo

Master Clarence Croft,
9 Willow St.,
Halifax, N.

A letter to Master Clarence (Clary) Croft, aged 8, 1960.

Nova Scotians have a deserved reputation for generosity when it comes to providing Christmas cheer to those less fortunate than themselves. It's a tradition that goes back to our earliest days. The *Nova Scotia Gazette and Weekly Chronicle*, December 16, 1788, carried the following notice: "On Sunday, the 7th instant, a charity sermon was preached at St Paul's, by the Right Reverend Bishop of Nova Scotia, for clothing the poor children of the Sunday Schools established in this town…It is expected that the clothing will [be] ready to be delivered by Christmas."

The tradition of providing for those less fortunate than ourselves continues with the annual food bank shows sponsored by various media, including the Canadian Broadcasting Corporation, and the Atlantic Television Network's *Christmas Daddies Telethon*, a Maritime province-wide event to raise funds to provide Christmas gifts to needy children. Conceived in 1964 by staff members Jim Hill and Jack Dalton, the show has become a Maritime Canadian tradition and has raised millions of dollars.

I was always blessed with an abundance of Christmas treats. My family didn't have a lot of money, but we were well provided for. My parents could even afford to have us children send out our own Christmas cards. I remember the excitement of going to the mailbox and finding a card addressed to "Master Clary Croft." It was the only time of the year I got mail.

The first Christmas card was created in England, and posted on December 9, 1842, or 1843. Designed by J. C. Horsley, it was printed on stiff paper with the simple message: "A Merry Christmas and a Happy New Year." It depicts a scene of adults and children raising their glasses in a Yuletide toast and, although a thousand copies were printed, only one has survived to this day. It has an honoured place at the Victoria and Albert Museum in London. Before the cards appeared in England, "Xmas pieces," were made by school boys to show their advanced penmanship. These letters were frequently decorated with borders of holly and mistletoe.

The early cards featured birds, animals, and nature motifs; religious iconography didn't appear until much later, as it wasn't considered suitable for such a secular activity. When postcards became popular at the end of the nineteenth century, the novelty or joke card appeared, but beautifully-designed sentimental cards with intricate cut-outs were also popular.

Manufacturers were constantly looking for ways to make their cards more appealing and early on, their design included the addition of artificial snow called "shiny flakes," which were actual pieces of ground glass glued to the paper's surface. In the 1950s, the Canadian Post Office asked card manufacturers to stop using ground glass as artificial snow because it fouled up the stamping machines. So they came up with something called "diamond dust," which has since been replaced by a plastic compound.

Christmas cards have undergone many changes. They are one of the best indicators of current trends and styles: Art Deco in the 1920s, themes in support of the troops in the 1940s, and cards featuring the ubiquitous family photos from the 1950s onward. In all eras, the historical image card has remained popular. Scenes of Victorian Christmases are still the most popular Christmas card images.

Card designers market to women, who purchase eighty per cent of all Christmas cards in North America. But, we're starting to see some unique and, some might say, disturbing trends in cards. Along with the simple "Baby's First Christmas," you can now find cards celebrating your Christmas divorce, or how about "Merry Christmas—You're Fired!" Some people might ever prefer those kinds of cards to the annual "Christmas Letter." You either love 'em or hate 'em. Even people who send them apologize in the first paragraph but make the plea that its easier to type the news once than write the same thing over and over again. And with today's computer graphics, it's now quite easy to send off a professional-looking message complete with photos.

Steve Murphy, Santa Claus and Scrooge from a Christmas Daddies telethon.

But each new innovation presents a new problem. How do you display these things? In the case of e-cards, do you print them off or just read them and press delete? Will we see the day when we no longer have cards taped around the door frames or strung on cords around the house? We've already begun to gather the folks around the VCR to see the latest video message from family members who have moved away or check out the web-cam for a live Christmas message. The technology is new but the need to have innovative ways to say Merry Christmas is not. Take for example this excerpt from the *South Shore Record* for December 16, 1937: "For the past few seasons there has been a growing custom of sending Christmas & New Year's greetings by telegram…Business firms are also taking advantage of the service to send…greetings to their patrons." So, you see, what was considered novel in 1937 is old hat today. You just can't keep ahead of technology.

Christmas decorations have evolved from simple, nature-inspired displays to high-tech laser lights beaming seasonal greetings into the sky. For years, people relied on natural products to decorate their home and churches. Fruits and nuts represented abundance, and evergreen boughs harkened back to a time when green branches were brought into homes as a symbol of the renewal of life after a long winter. And although this tradition was of pagan origins, decorating with evergreens soon became an acceptable way of adorning the Christian sanctuary. Take this Nova Scotian example from the diary of Liverpool's Simeon Perkins: "Monday December 24, 1804…daughter at the chapel…dressing it with green bows for Xmas."

The Perkins family probably had no idea they were upholding a custom as old as those followed by the Druids. In the pre-Christian era, holly was the symbol of male fertility. Christians altered the symbolism so the holly branches represented the crown of thorns placed upon Christ's head at his trial and crucifixion. The red berries represent the blood of Christ and the plant is scrubby as punishment for allowing itself to be used to make the thorny crown. Some believe it bad luck to bring

Xmas Card, c. 1953, sent to Clary by Mrs. Henry Archibald, Sherbrooke. Inscribed: To my little boy, This is you and me going for gas in our little car. Hope Santa is good to you and you have lots of toys.

holly into the house before Christmas Eve and that it should be removed by January 6.

The ancient Druids also worshiped with mistletoe, a symbol of peace and prosperity. Pieces of it were hung over the door as a sign that old grievances were gone and both men and women would kiss under the plant as a sign of peace. Mistletoe and holly can now be found packaged in plastic bags, ready to be used in holiday displays. If you buy the plastic stuff it will last several generations. But although artificial evergreen is very realistic, it just doesn't have the smell of balsam or fir. And those aerosol spray cans of pine scent—forget 'em. Give me a few boughs of the real thing any day!

Years ago, market vendors in Nova Scotia would haul huge loads of evergreens to the larger urban centres. In the Halifax area, this was a substantial source of winter income, especially for many Acadian and African Nova Scotian families, who sold individual bundles, swags, and garlands at the city market. Some of the descendants of those original sellers can still be found at the Halifax Farmers Market during the Christmas season. They sell boughs and branches of various kinds, in addition to spray-painted gold or silver branches and beautiful bunches of rosehips and other red winter berries that all go under the name of holly.

Styles of decoration come and go. Many people like what they believe to be an "old-fashioned" look. From the mid-nineteenth century up until the 1950s, most Nova Scotian homes were festooned with paper streamers draped from one corner to the next forming a swagged cross on the ceiling. And holding court in the centre: a paper bell! When I was a child, streamers and bells were the only store-bought decorations that were common. Today the Christmas decoration market is flooded with a myriad of items: from ceramic statues to complete sets of Christmas china; from a plastic baby Jesus in the manger to a musical crèche that plays eight different carols. The list is endless. And, lest you be too quick to judge, remember—one person's kitsch is another's treasure.

Since the 1950s, we've seen a new Christmas decorating trend. It used to be that a house might have candles in the windows and, when electricity became common, a few lighted wreaths shining through the winter night. But with the post-war housing developments, cheap electricity and a desire to show off, houses became showplaces for outside decorations, especially strings of coloured lights. Besides, in Halifax, the Nova Scotia Light & Power Company had a magical display of automated figures and glittering lights in the basement of their store on Barrington Street. Every child wanted their house to be lit up like that, and many parents aspired to show off their artistic talents by complying. The number of homes illuminated (and the millions of bulbs used) reached dizzying heights in the 1960s, but collapsed in the 1970s when power rates soared.

But, the tradition was here to stay. After all, people had to try and maintain at least a few lighted decorations so another annual rite could be observed: the drive to see the lights! Families would pile into their cars and converge on the wealthier neighborhoods to ooh and aah at the spectacular displays. By the 1990s, people were once again covering their homes with lights, only this time the manufacturers had come out with "cascade lights" that could make any home appear frosted with tinkling stars.

Now, in the twenty-first century, even the traditional has gone high-tech. Each year, historic Sherbrooke Village decorates its Victorian buildings and attracts thousands of visitors to see the illuminated Christmas displays. It's oddly beautiful—these classic nineteenth-century Nova Scotian houses outlined in electric points of light. I wonder what the original inhabitants would make of it? They'd probably take it all in stride. After all, it was during the Victorian era that Nova Scotians saw the introduction of many of the traditions we now associate with an old-fashioned Christmas, including our most popular Christmas decoration—the Christmas tree.

In fact, some people believe the first Christmas tree in Canada originated in 1846 when Barbara Pryor erected a tree at Coburg Cottage in Halifax. It was decorated with coloured candles in glass holders, glass ornaments from Germany, cookies, candies, cranberry chains, popcorn chains, small gifts, rosehips and bits of ribbon. Mrs. Pryor was following a Christian tradition from her German heritage and probably knew little of the symbol's pagan origins.

Pre-Christian Europeans used to cut down evergreen trees in late winter and bring them indoors. Like the use of evergreen boughs, a living tree was the symbol of the surety of continued life. The Druids tied fruit and attached tapers to evergreen tree branches in honour of their god Woden. Pagan Romans decorated living trees with bits of metal and images of the fertility god Bacchus.

A legend explaining how the evergreen tree came to be adopted as a Christian symbol is the story of a miracle attributed to Saint Boniface. To show the power of the Christian faith, Boniface cut down an oak tree in the presence of some newly-baptized Christians. The tree was considered sacred to the former pagans, but when the saint split it in four pieces he revealed an evergreen tree growing from the center of the stump.

A more common legend is that Martin Luther brought a living tree home from the forest and decorated it with lighted candles to symbolize the Christ child as the everlasting light of the world. He was probably following a Christian custom that dates back to western Germany in the sixteenth century. On December 24, also known as Adam and Eve Day, people would bring evergreen Paradeisbaum (Paradise Trees) into homes and decorate them with apples and, in some cases, sacramental wafers. One of the earliest documented accounts of a decorated tree comes from Strasbourg, in Alsace, in 1605, which had cookies and candies hanging from the branches.

Over the centuries, decorated trees became

common Christmas symbols in Germany, and when Prince Albert of Saxe-Coburg-Gotha married Victoria of England, he brought the tradition to Windsor Castle, where the royal family enjoyed their first tree in 1844. Once the idea of a Christmas tree received royal sanction, it didn't take long for many of the Queen's subjects to follow, including Barbara Pryor in 1846.

But not everyone adopted the custom. For a long while it seems only those with means could afford any of the commercial decorations associated with decorating a tree. It was more common to see stores and social organizations have a decorated tree that people visited.

In December 1876, the Halifax *Morning Chronicle* reported that: "Marter's Drug Store, 172 Granville Street, will have a dressed tree that will have candles and some regular customers will receive free gifts."

Even into the first few decades of the twentieth century there were some families in Nova Scotia that didn't put up a Christmas tree. My father, who grew up in St. Mary's River, doesn't remember having a tree at home in the 1920s and 30s. He does remember travelling down the road to visit his aunt and uncle to see their Christmas tree, a novelty for many children in the community. But Dad's family just didn't have the money to spend on Christmas decorations.

However, anyone with the funds to purchase decorations could find an abundance of them in the shops. From the late Victorian era to the present day, new forms of baubles and twinkling decorations are added to the Christmas tree-gilding list every year. There was also the option of making decorations at home from scraps of this and that, but a plethora of manufactured goods was always on hand for the holiday decorator with cash.

Artificial icicles, made from thin strips of silver foil, were first made and sold in Nuremberg, Germany, in 1878. By 1880 German Christmas decoration manufacturers were producing garlands of "angel hair," made of spun glass. It had to be handled very carefully because the sharp glass filaments could give a nasty cut. In the 1890s garlands of tinsel became popular. Made of silver-plated copper wire (produced by a secret process originally developed in France for decorating military uniforms) the garland was bunched and clipped to give a bushy effect. However many of these metallic decorations tarnished and had to be replaced after only a few years of use. Then, in the 1920s, American manufacturers developed lead-foil icicles that didn't tarnish. In the 1960s, because of the danger of lead poisoning, lead foil icicles were replaced by Mylar, a polyester film. Mylar was also a lot cheaper to produce.

Glass ornaments produced by specialty manufacturers in Germany were some of the first commercial decorations used on the tree, and the early examples show that although some were free-formed, or mouth blown, many were made in moulds that produced heavy, but consistent and uniform shapes. For decades these classic German ornaments were rare and prized additions to the family's Christmas tree. But it was the great

American consumer market that produced an unparalleled popularity in glass tree ornaments.

In the late nineteenth century, Frank Woolworth, reluctantly at first, began selling blown-glass ornaments in his fourteen stores. Within a decade he was ordering two hundred thousand annually. By the turn of the century, glass blowers were producing all kinds of shapes for his outlets, especially fruits, story book characters, and fish. These were frequently hand painted or lacquered in bright colours. Then, in 1910 ,Sears began advertising and selling glass ornaments by mail. This meant even people in remote areas had access to exotic glass balls and figures for the tree. But even then, almost all of the glass ornaments sold were individually made and decorated by hand. It wasn't until 1939 that the Corning Company became the first company to mass-produce machine-made ornaments and balls.

World War Two caused the Corning Company to alter some of their manufacturing techniques. Because of restrictions in the availability of metals, they couldn't obtain the "silvering" for their ornaments, so they began manufacturing clear glass bulbs painted with stripes, and by the end of the war, cardboard caps had replaced metal ones.

But, it is the illumination of the Christmas tree that has seen the greatest number of changes. At first people used wax candles held on with metal holders. It was a great occasion when the tree was lit and the entire family gathered around (probably with full water buckets at the ready) and enjoyed the brief spectacle. The first electric Christmas tree lights were displayed on a tree in New York in 1882. They were developed by the new Edison Electric Company. By the 1890s General Electric began to promote Christmas-tree lights. They looked very much like small clear light bulbs and had to be plugged in from the ceiling fixture and draped over the tree. The company didn't add colour to their lights until 1910.

From the 1920s to the 1950s, Japan was the leader in tree light manufacturing. Some of the most popular shapes came from the current cartoon characters of the day: Little Orphan Annie, Popeye and Dick Tracy. Many of these "made in Japan" models are easily recognized by collectors today because the characters, even Santa, have distinctly Asian facial features.

The 1930s saw the introduction of flashing lights and in 1945, bubble lights, invented by Carl Otis, an accountant at Montgomery Ward Company added a new twist to tree luminescence. The bulbs contained methylene chloride, a liquid that will boil at the low temperature of a tree light. In the 1970s flashing lights, marketed as "twinkle lights," were back in style, only this time in "midget" form. They became the biggest sellers in the history of tree lights.

I foresee the time when trees won't need lights at all; in fact, you won't even need a tree. You'll have a Christmas tree hologram in your room. Just add a little spray of pine scented air freshener and your cheeks will glow with the yuletide spirit. But then again, people may want to return to the more traditional kinds of trees Nova Scotians enjoyed in the past.

It seems many people go in for theme trees, but most of the ones I remember from my childhood, both at home and at my friends' homes, were decorated with a mélange of styles and collection of ornaments handed down through the generations. But, everyone had their own unique look. Some people always chose a spindly tree with lots of space between the branches for draping swags; others looked for the thickest, most luxurious fir so the ornaments could lay on the surface. The topper for the tree was definitely a strong personal choice: a star or an angel? Was the tree secured with a metal stand or by crosses of wooden boards? Was it bare underneath or did it have the luxury of a tree skirt? One attractive traditional way of decorating around the base of the tree in Lunenburg County was with a blanket of cotton wool snow underneath (frequently quilt batting) and a farmyard scene complete with oxen, surrounded by a white picket fence.

Then, there are the traditions surrounding the actual decoration of the tree which, for many families included the annual "fight to untangle the lights." While some people hold tree decorating parties and make it a real family affair, others maintain the decoration must be done by the parents after the children have gone to bed on Christmas eve. The first time the young ones see the decorated tree is on Christmas morning!

Whatever the traditions may be, it's a safe bet that unless you own your own woodlot the Christmas tree you decorate each year comes from a tree farm. In

Traditional Lunenburg County farm scene beneath the Xmas tree.

Nova Scotia, tree farming has become a major industry—one that has been around for longer than most people think.

On December 3, 1898, the *Presbyterian Witness* announced that "Another new industry has started in Yarmouth—the shipment of spruce Christmas trees to Boston." It has been a thriving industry ever since. Nova Scotia is now known as "The Christmas Tree Province" and Lunenburg County as "The Balsam Fir Christmas Tree Capital of the World."

We've also been involved with a tradition that was brought about because of the good will and generosity of the people of New England after the Halifax Explosion in 1917. When they heard of the horrific destruction and loss of lives, they sent medical supplies and personnel to the rescue. As a token of our gratitude, the province sends one of its largest and finest Christmas trees to Boston where it is adorned with thousands of lights and "switched on" in a ceremony that has become a Boston ritual.

Although Martin Luther is credited with the custom of putting lighted candles on a tree at Christmas, Christians had been using candles in their religious celebrations centuries before they appeared on a tree. Many people believe a candle to be a significant part of Christian iconography. The wax represents Christ's body, the wick his soul, and the flame his divinity.

Beeswax candles are frequently used in the church because of the tradition that bees come from paradise. Candles can also be scented with essential oils, including the waxy oil from bayberries. An interesting belief associated with this is that sweethearts who are separated at Christmas can light bayberry candles and the scent will reach the other if they are truly in love.

Many Acadian homes in Nova Scotia have a lighted candle in each window to show the Christ child a safe haven. The old people would never use store-bought candles; they made their own in special moulds saved for the holidays. It was especially important to have these candles in the windows on Christmas Eve.

A more secular Acadian tradition once popular in the Tatamagouche area was playing card games on Christmas Eve—especially forty-fives. Helen Creighton learned about this custom from several Acadian and Mi'kmaw informants.

Other popular Christmas pastimes included games of chance and skill. An example from the *Pictou Advocate*, December 24, 1897, carried this notice about one such event at Cape John: "The Skinner Brothers intend holding a shooting match on Christmas afternoon. Their prizes will be a rifle, a pistol, a number of geese, and other articles."

More refined customs, still very popular today, are church and community Christmas teas and bazaars. And most people attend at least one Christmas concert either at their place of worship or their children's school. The universal uniform of an old bathrobe for a shepherd's cloak and a strand of tinsel garland for an angel's halo are images many of us remember from our childhood.

My mother tells me I was singing almost before I could talk, so it was natural for me to be involved in every Christmas pageant and concert at Sunday School and grade school. However, one of my first public appearances almost ended in disaster and may have nipped my promising career in the bud. I would have been around five and my friend, Linda Scott, was a couple of years older. We were to sing a duet at our Christmas concert, which was held in the basement of the Presbyterian Church in Sherbrooke. I'm sure we were dressed to the nines. We took our places, the piano accompaniment began and we both started giggling. I don't remember if we even got through the song, or what the song was for that matter. I have some kind of residual memory of being taken off the stage. I know that I've blocked that part of the scenario from my mind and poor Linda probably made the decision then and there to end her promising entertainment career as well. In later years, I was always a featured performer at Christmas concerts, but its nice to remember how even the mighty can be reduced to social ridicule. And that, I'm sure, is just one of thousands of disaster stories from Christmas concert lore.

How many juvenile elocutionists were letter-perfect before the big event only to need repeated prompting from the teacher in the wings? How many understudies have had to step in and raise the letter X in the M-E-R-R-Y X-M-A-S message when the original child came down with the flu? How many little boys performed with the indignity of an unzipped fly? How many little girls had their personal appearances dramatically altered by an unsuccessful home perm the night before their major debut? Who knows, maybe Christmas concerts are a subliminal way to discourage children from pursuing a life on the stage.

But I hope what most children remember about their Christmas concerts is the fun and excitement of rehearsal; of peeking through the curtain to find mom and dad sitting proudly in the front row; of delivering their four-line Christmas verse in syllables that even the gap left by two missing front teeth couldn't blur; and singing much-loved Christmas songs, even if the music teacher told them, "Since you're a crow dear, and will never be a bluebird, just mouth the words!" Sorry, not tonight lady! The Christmas concert was one time you could lift your tuneless little voice and join the angelic chorus. After all, singing along with Christmas songs is one of life's great pleasures.

Nova Scotians have a great reputation as singers and Christmas gives us a chance to shine. And, one was never limited to the standard holiday repertoire. At Chezzetcook the men would sit opposite one another at a table holding a handkerchief between them and sing the old traditional ballads.

Many of the Christmas favourites we have come to know weren't even around in our ancestors' time. Take, as example, a Christmas classic "O Little Town of Bethlehem." Phillips Brooks, of Massachusetts, wrote those familiar lines as a poem while visiting the holy land in 1867. And although Lewis H. Redner wrote a melody for it the following Christmas Eve, it took another twenty-five years for it to become a common carol in hymnals. The Victorian age saw the development of sheet music publication which led to the popularization of these new Christmas carols.

For some Nova Scotians, carols were reserved for church. Christmas gatherings were often seen as a time for secular music and dancing. At Port la Tour they played harmonicas, tambourines, and violins. At Mahone Bay, an auto harp and triangle were added to these instruments. Music and step-dancing were often so lively that the party telephone lines were left open for the neighbors to enjoy. At Chezzetcook the people danced plain sets, lancers, polkas and waltzes. At Bear River, some Mi'kmaq told Helen Creighton that they enjoyed Christmas celebrations by dancing old-fashioned eights and ending with war dances. Lawson Innes of Peggy's Cove told her: "We always had two or three fiddles and would sing by-times, and occasionally would make a song up. Rube Dobbin could do that; he was our santa claw. We made our own decorations and children hung their stockings all round the chimney corner, oh my, mighty yes!"

Not only did we enjoy our music at home, we frequently shared it with others in the province and even on a national scale. From the *South Shore Record* (Mahone Bay) for December 16, 1937, comes the following announcement: "The Lunenburg Glee Club has again brought honor to its native town, as it has been chosen to take part in the National broadcast on Christmas Day." The broadcast featured twenty-five singers and an accompanist playing the pipe organ. Most fittingly for Lunenburg, the performance included two songs in German: "Silent Night" and "O Tennebaum," as well as "O Little Town of Bethlehem."

Christmas music broadcasts have become a traditional part of African Nova Scotian culture. In 1931, children from the Nova Scotia Home for Coloured Children were taken to radio station CHNS in Halifax. There they performed live in efforts to raise funds for the institution. Their repertoire included some traditional African Nova Scotian folk songs, but was made up primarily of standard Christmas tunes. The broadcast proved so popular that soon the show was being done live from the home and had the addition of adult performers, all helping to raise funds for the home. The fund-raising broadcasts continue today, only now the medium used is television.

Radio station CHNS also gave Nova Scotians in Halifax and the surrounding area live Christmas broadcasts from the Simpsons department store. In the early years, these included live orchestras and professional singers, while later on the music was often provided by Dick Fry at the Hammond Organ and the singers were store employees. It was a regular holiday tradition in my house to tune in and sing along with the Christmas songs, especially since the lyrics had been provided through the local newspaper. It was probably the biggest Christmas Carol sing-a-long the province ever had!

Christmas Carols and songs tend to become fairly standardized. That is, until you get beyond the first line. After that, it's everyone for themselves. They are so universally known that we tend to forget that regional and even cultural variants can be found, which is certainly the case for interesting Nova Scotian variants of well-known songs. Thanks to the folk song collection of Dr. Helen Creighton and the people who shared their songs with her, we have unique examples of Christmas songs of our own. Perhaps the oldest song on that list is "The Cherry Tree Carol."

This lovely old carol has its origins in one of the miracle stories found in the Gospel of Pseudo-Matthew, Chapter 20 in the books of the Apocrypha. It goes back at least to the Middle Ages and is found in the Coventry Miracle Plays. Helen Creighton collected a fragment of the carol from Mrs. Annie C. Wallace in Halifax. But, her most complete version comes from the singing of William Riley of Cherry Brook. The written notes cannot convey the beauty and integrity Mr. Riley brings to this song. He employs the West African falsetto whoop in his vocal styling that gives his particular variant a rich African Nova Scotian component. I included a contemporary version on my recording "A Maritime Christmas Celebration," but the original recording can be heard on a CD I co-produced for the Black Cultural Centre of Nova Scotia and the Canadian Broadcasting Corporation, called "Lord You Brought Me A Might Long Way: An African Nova Scotian Musical Journey." (For the music see Helen Creighton, *Traditional Songs from Nova Scotia*, page 34.)

The Cherry Tree Carol

Then Joseph took Mary up on his right knee,
Saying, "Mary, won't you tell me when the birth day shall be?"
Saying, "Mary, won't you tell me when the birth day shall be?"

"The birth day shall be on that old Christmas night,
When the angels in the glory rejoice at the sight,
When the angels in the glory rejoice at the sight."

Oh Mary walked in the garden just like a little child,
Saying, "Give me some cherries for I am beguiled,"
Saying, "Give me some cherries for I am beguiled."

Joseph said to Mary, "I give thee no cherries,
Let the man give you cherries who did you beguile,
Let the man give you cherries who did you beguile."

Then the tree spoke unto her and it began to bow,
(The tree hearkened to him and it began to bow,) [alternative line]
Saying, "Mary, gather cherries from the uttermost limb."
Saying, "Mary, gather cherries from the uttermost limb."

Another traditional song in the Helen Creighton's collection is "The Joys (or Blessings) of Mary."

Dr. Creighton collected two different variants of this ancient carol. The first was from Miss Norma Smith who presented Helen with a version sung by her "Grandpa Saunders," who used to sing the song every Christmas Day. He was born in Britain in 1833 and immigrated to Canada where, according to Miss Smith, "He would only sing this on Christmas Day, no matter how much we would coax to have it at other times. ... Because of the demi-semi-quavers at the end, he said only an Englishman could sing it." Compare Mr. Saunders' version to that later collected from William Riley, the amazing African Nova Scotian singer from Cherry Brook. He titled the song "The Blessings of Mary " and, unlike Mr. Saunders, Mr. Riley's daughter Rose told me her father would sing the song any time of the year.

The Joys of Mary

(Sanders version. For the music see Helen Creighton, Traditional Songs from Nova Scotia, page 275)

The first great joy that Mary had it was the joy of one,
To know her own Son Jesus was God's only Son,
Was God's only Son, good man, and blessed may He be,
Father, Son and Holy Ghost, to all eternity.

Now the next great joy that Mary had it was the joy of two,

To hear her own Son Jesus read the Bible through,
Read the Bible through, good man, and blessed may He be,
Father, Son and Holy Ghost, to all eternity.

The next great joy that Mary had it was the joy of three,
To see her own Son Jesus make the blind to see,
Make the blind to see, good man, and blessed may He be,
Father, Son and Holy Ghost, to all eternity.

The next great joy that Mary had it was the joy of four,
To see her own Son Jesus enrich the humble poor,
Enrich the humble poor, good man, and blessed may He be,
Father, Son and Holy Ghost, to all eternity.

Now the next great joy that Mary had it was the joy of five,
To see her own Son Jesus make the dead alive,
Make the dead alive, good man, and blessed may He be,
Father, Son and Holy Ghost, to all eternity.

Now the next great joy that Mary had it was the joy of six,
To see her own Son Jesus become a crucifix,
Become a crucifix, good man, and blessed may He be,
Father, Son and Holy Ghost, to all eternity.

The next great joy that Mary had it was the joy of seven,
To see her own Son Jesus send a thief to heaven,
Send a thief to heaven, good man, and blessed may He be,
Father, Son and Holy Ghost, to all eternity.

The next great joy that Mary had it was the joy of eight,
To see her own Son Jesus make the crooked straight,
Make the crooked straight, good man, and blessed may He be,
Father, Son and Holy Ghost, to all eternity.

The next great joy that Mary had it was the joy of nine,
To see her own Son Jesus turn water into wine,
Turn water into wine, good man, and blessed may He be,
Father, Son and Holy Ghost, to all eternity.

The next great joy that Mary had it was the joy of ten,
To see her own Son Jesus feed five thousand men,
Feed five thousand men, good man, and blessed may He be,
Father, Son and Holy Ghost, to all eternity.

The next great joy that Mary had it was the joy of eleven,
To see her own Son Jesus descend up into heaven,
Descend up into heaven, good man, and blessed may He be,
Father, Son and Holy Ghost, to all eternity.

The next great joy that Mary had it, it made her heart stand still,
To know her own Son Jesus had worked His Father's will,
Had worked His Father's will, good man, and blessed may He be,
Father, Son and Holy Ghost, to all eternity.

The Blessings of Mary

(Riley version. For the music see Helen Creighton, Traditional Songs from Nova Scotia, page 172)

Oh, the very first blessing Sister Mary had, she had the blessing of one,
To think on her own son, Jesus, who suckled at the breast so young,
Who suckled at the breast so, I believe it, who suckled at the breast so young,
Who suckled at the breast so young.

The very next blessing Sister Mary had, she had the blessing of two,
To think of her own son, Jesus, could read the Bible through,
Could read the Bible through, I believe it, could read the Bible through,
Could read the Bible through.

The very next blessing Sister Mary had, she had the blessing of three,
To think on her own son, Jesus, could set poor sinners free,
Could set poor sinners free, I believe it, could set poor sinners free,
Could set poor sinners free.

The very next blessing Sister Mary had, she had the blessing of four,
To think on her own son, Jesus, could turn the rich to poor,
Could turn the rich to poor, I believe it, could turn the rich to poor,
Could turn the rich to poor.

The very next blessing Sister Mary had, she had the blessing of five,
To think on her own son, Jesus, could turn the dead to live,
Could turn the dead to live, I believe it, could turn the dead to live,
Could turn the dead to live.

The very next blessing Sister Mary had, she had the blessing of six,
To think on her own son, Jesus, who had all things well fixed,
Who had all things well fixed, I believe it, who had all things well fixed,
Who had all things well fixed.

The very next blessing Sister Mary had, she had the blessing of seven,
To think on her own son, Jesus, He did ring the bells of heaven,
He did ring the bells of heaven, I believe it, He did ring the bells of heaven,
He did ring the bells of heaven.

The very next blessing Sister Mary had, she had the blessing of eight,
To think on her own son, Jesus, could make the crooked way straight,
Could make the crooked way straight, I believe it, could make the crooked way straight,
Could make the crooked way straight.

The very next blessing Sister Mary had, she had the blessing of nine,
To think on her own son, Jesus, He did turn the water to wine,
He did turn the water to wine, I believe it, He did turn the water to wine,
He did turn the water to wine.

The very next blessing Sister Mary had, she had the blessing of ten,
To think on her own son, Jesus, did write without a pen,
Did write without a pen, I believe it, did write without a pen,
Did write without a pen.

The very next blessing Sister Mary had, she had the blessing of eleven,
To think on her own son, Jesus, did ring the bells of heaven,
Did ring the bells of heaven, I believe it, did ring the bells of heaven,
Did ring the bells of heaven.

The very next blessing Sister Mary had, she had the blessing of twelve,
To think on her own son, Jesus, who conquered when He fell,
Who conquered when He fell, I believe it, who conquered when He fell,
Who conquered when He fell.

Mother, how still the babe do lie, cannot discern His breath,
Neither behold His mortal eye, pray tell me the baby is dead,
Pray tell me the baby is dead, I believe it, pray tell me the baby is dead,
Pray tell me the baby is dead.

Husband dear, you are so near, fled away and gone,
My backstay is taken away, and I am left alone,
And I am left alone, I believe it, and I am left alone,
And I am left alone.

There is also a fascinating Gaelic Christmas song from the Helen Creighton collection. It is sung to the Gaelic melody for the song "Ho Ro Mo Nighean Donn Bhòidheach" (Ho Ro My Nut Brown Maiden). The translation was given to Helen by the Reverend J.D.N. MacDonald of Woodlawn, Nova Scotia, who told Dr. Creighton that it wasn't a rarity to have an English verse or two interspersed with the Gaelic verses. This song doesn't seem to have a formal title. (For the music see *Fad Air Falbh As Innse Gall: Beyond the Hebrides* by Donald A. Fergusson, page 180.)

Mu'n àm seo dhe na bhliadhna,
Tha "Santa Claus" cho fialaidh,
Is' daoine s'iad fo fhiabhras,
Ag iarraidh chun na craoibh.

Bhi dèanabh "time" do phàisdean,
Mar chleacheadh anns an àite,
Bi cluiche, 'us ceòl gàire,
Ri fhaicinn air gach taobh.

'S e bu choir bhi taingeal,
Luchd sgoil na h-aibhne Frangeach,
Dòmhnul 's e na chean' orra,
Cumail suas a chliu.

Bha Dòmhnul dhuibse ag innse,
Gu robh a chlann cho dileas,
Air leughadh agus sgriobhadh,
'Sa h-uile ni air tùs.
When Donald Fraser is the fireman
The heat it would surprise you.
R.J says he is frying,
He sits down near the stove.

Is aithne dhuibh a chairdean,
Nach eil sinn math air bardachd,
Cead soraidh dhuibh an dràsda,
Agus bliadhna mhath ùr.

(J.D.N. MacDonald's translation: "At this time of year Santa Claus is generous. Men are under a fever going to the tree making a good time for the children after the custom of the place with fun and music and laughter on every side. The ones who ought to be thankful are the people of French River. Donald, the teacher, was at their head keeping up the custom and telling that the children were so faithful at reading, writing and all other things. Although you people know by this time that I am not much of a bard, we are wishing for you now a happy New Year.")

When I was working on my recording of Maritime Canadian Christmas songs and lore, I incorporated a traditional Cape Breton Acadian belief collected by Sister Mary Fraser into one of my own compositions. I called it "Song of the Oxen," from Sister Mary's reference to the ancient belief that certain animals, including oxen, are given the power of speech at Christmas as a reward for blowing their warm breath on the Christ child and guarding Him as he lay in the manger. She wrote about a schoolmaster who took great pride in his knowledge of Latin and decided to test the belief by listening in on the animals' conversation. (He naturally assumed the animals would speak Latin.) He wasn't disappointed, for according to Sister Fraser's account, on the stroke of midnight the cock in a soprano voice sang, "Christus natus est! Christus natus est!" The ox replied, asking, "ubi?, ubi?" The answer from the ass, in his basso profundo voice, was "Bethlehem! Bethlehem!"

This tradition of oxen speaking at Christmas is not only known among Acadians. Folklore collectors have also found the belief among other cultural and ethnic groups, especially African Nova Scotians and people of German decent in and around Lunenburg County.

Oxen (castrated cattle) are one of the oldest beasts of burden and one of the first animals to be domesticated. They were once very common in Nova Scotia because they were considered better than horses for hauling in wooded areas with a lot of stumps and rocks. An ox will pull slowly and pick his steps in a unhurried plodding way, while a horse might start up quickly and get skittish if he is having difficulties. Also, it was perfectly acceptable to eat an oxen after it had outlived its usefulness, while this was never done with horses.

As late as 1918, it was not usual in Halifax to see sleds pulled by single oxen and, in rural areas, individual beasts or teams were commonly used in the woods and fields until the introduction of tractors in the 1940s. In fact, during World War Two, they were considered essential animals and one needed permission from the governing powers in Ottawa to dispose of an ox. However, unless circumstances were dire, most people kept their prized oxen as long as they could. They are gentle, handsome beasts, still held in great affection by many of their handlers. One rarely sees working oxen today, but displays of their amazing size and strength can still be seen at such events as the International Ox Pull at the South Shore Exhibition in Bridgewater, which is the premiere event for competitors.

It may be because for so many years oxen were part of the daily life for Nova Scotians that the traditional belief of their powers of speech survived as long as they did. Certainly, the folklore surrounding their mystic qualities are known in many cultures. There is as Iranian myth of a great ox from whose blood sprang all useful herbs and animals. In Italy, ox horns are used to protect people from the evil eye.

In Nova Scotia, Helen Creighton collected many variants of Christmas oxen-speaking legend, including some where the creatures also fell to their knees at midnight on Christmas Eve. But, along with the belief comes an admonishment. You must never try to hear or see them doing any of these magical rites. If you do, you will die within the coming year. Helen was told that one man listened and heard the oxen saying that tomorrow they would be hauling wood to make their master's coffin. He died the next day!

Perhaps it was better to be ignorant of the activities of your oxen, or at least of their language. According to one story Dr. Creighton collected, a man from Seabright bought a pair of oxen from a man in Lunenburg. On Christmas Eve he went to the barn to see if the legend of talking oxen was true. Sure enough, he heard them speak but, unlike the Acadian oxen from Cape Breton who spoke Latin, his oxen conversed in German. Since he didn't understand the language of the Lunenburg County "Dutch" (or Deutch) oxen, he was spared.

Lunenburg County is also the primary place of celebration for one of the most interesting traditional folk customs in the province. "Belsnickling" is a practice similar to mumming or mummering, when celebrants dress in disguises and visit homes to receive treats and make merry. There are distinct regional variants that make them unique to Nova Scotia, including "Kris Kringling" (at Port La Tour) and "Santa Clausing" or "Santy Clausing" (in Shelburne County). Variations of belsnickling are practiced throughout the world.

"Santa Clausing" or "Santy Clausing" was the name given to the festivities in Shelburne County and its environs. Celebrations would begin on Christmas Eve and continue until Epiphany. People prepared for weeks in advance. Those going from door to door were called "Santa Clauses."They dressed in costumes made from old clothes and carried a bag of cakes and sugar cookies, called "santys." Poems and stories were recited about some local person or event, playlets were presented in the kitchens and parlours visited, and there was music and step-dancing. In addition to receiving "santys" from the visiting "Santa Clauses," plates of the sugar cookies were placed out in the homes so the visitors could help themselves if their stock got low. Marion Robertson tells us the custom of "Santa Clausing" was practiced on Cape Sable Island and in Lockport long after it died out in other communities.

The custom of belsnickling also almost completely died out, but has seen a revival of sorts in Lunenburg County. The term belsnickle comes from the German *peltznickle*. In German tradition, Saint Nicholas brings gifts to children and two of his best-known assistants are Knecht Ruprecht (Servant Rupert) and the Belsnickle or Pelznickle, meaning Furry Nicholas, referring to his animal hide and fur-clad appearance. While both characters were helpers and carried the additional responsibility of rewarding good children, they also punished children who were naughty and couldn't recite their prayers.

Helen Creighton collected numerous examples of belsnickling folklore and published them in *Folklore of Lunenburg County* in 1950. In 1971, folklorist Richard Bauman published additional material he collected in and around La Have in his work titled *Belsnickling in a Nova Scotia Community*.

While Richard found that, for the most part, it was the men and boys who participated as belsnicklers until shortly before the World War Two, he also noted that Helen Creighton found examples in Lunenburg County were women dressed as the Magi and carried gifts to distribute at the homes they visited. They were known as "Kris Kringles," which was also the name given to raisin cakes made and given out in several communities, including Rose Bay. The most common treats the belsnicklers could expect were cakes, cookies, doughnuts, apples, and occasionally in the later years, expensive oranges. Sometimes this was known as receiving "a bit of brouse." One woman told me she remembers her father setting out a card table for the belsnicklers who came to her home in Bridgewater in the 1950s. On it he would place stacks of coins and a few of these would be given to each belsnickling child when they visited the house.

In older times, children belsnickles were expected to kneel and say their prayers upon entering a house before they received treats, and, if a tree was present, they were then allowed to view it. An interesting dichotomy here is that children could be both belsnicklers and have the brunt of lore used against them. Naughty children were sometimes warned "the belsnicklers will get you" and adult belsnicklers sometimes used tails of unravelled rope to thrash the youngsters.

Unravelled rope was also used as part of the belsnicklers' costumes. Belsnicklers wore ox horns and hides, and sported beards and belts made from oakum and rope. They frequently carried ox bells or other noise-making items. Others wore old clothes or costumes they made up specially for the occasion. Many wore tall hats made of canvas or a stocking cap stuffed to make it stiff. Some dressed as grotesque women. Masks made of painted canvas were often worn to disguise the wearer's identity.

It was important to remain as incognito as possible, something not always easy to do in a small community where everyone knows your gait, stature, vocal tone and even your ordinary clothes. Helen Creighton was told if the people had no old clothes to spare, they turned their regular togs inside out.

Once they were allowed admittance to the house the belsnicklers sang songs, did crazy dances and generally acted the fool; some tried to kiss the women or sit on their laps. Others belsnickled with music from a mouth organ, but there was no singing— perhaps because their singing voices might give them away. It would have been unacceptable to turn them away and a drink of rum or other spirits was always a necessary offering.

Celebrations usually began immediately after dark on Christmas Eve. Years ago, at Peggy's Cove, people would belsnickle for an entire week, often into the sixth of January. Still others ended their revels on New Year's Eve and, if they had the means, would change their costumes from black to white. They were called New Year's Bucks. (See New Year's.)

In recent years the citizens of the town of Lunenburg have made attempts to revive the belsnickling traditions. It will be interesting to see how many of the old customs will be carried over into the twenty-first century and what new traditions will be made by today's belsnicklers. In any case, it will be most interesting for folklore researchers like myself.

On Corkum's Island they wouldn't go to the well after dark on Christmas Eve for fear it would turn the water into wine. (Creighton)

At Christmas Eve go to the cellar, turn around three times, look in the mirror, and you will see your future husband. (Creighton)

If you look in the mirror on Christmas Eve you will see the devil looking out. (Creighton)

Green Christmas—full graveyard, Green Christmas—white Easter. (Creighton)

BOXING DAY

DECEMBER 26

THE DAY AFTER CHRISTMAS is known in the Christian church as the Feast of St. Stephen, named in honour of the first Christian martyr. In the secular world, and society in general, it is called Boxing Day. There are a couple of possible origins for the term and, chances are, it is derived from a blending of both.

Sometime in the ninth century AD it became common for churches in Britain to open their alms boxes and distribute the funds to the poor on the day immediately following Christmas. But, Boxing Day may take its name from the custom of rewarding servants who had provided faithful service throughout the year. Most servants were required to work on Christmas. After all, they were responsible for making the holiday run smoothly for their masters. On December 26 many were allowed to return home to visit with their families and it was traditional for their employers to give them a box containing gifts and bonuses.

When I was a child, I thought the day was so named because it was the time when merchants took down their Christmas decorations and unsold inventory and put them away in boxes. I wasn't far off the mark. Today, most business conduct huge Boxing Day sales, where shrewd shoppers can take advantage of some amazing bargains. After all, the merchants don't want to hold the inventory over into the new year—especially Christmas merchandise. This trend has become so popular that many stores offer Boxing Week sales.

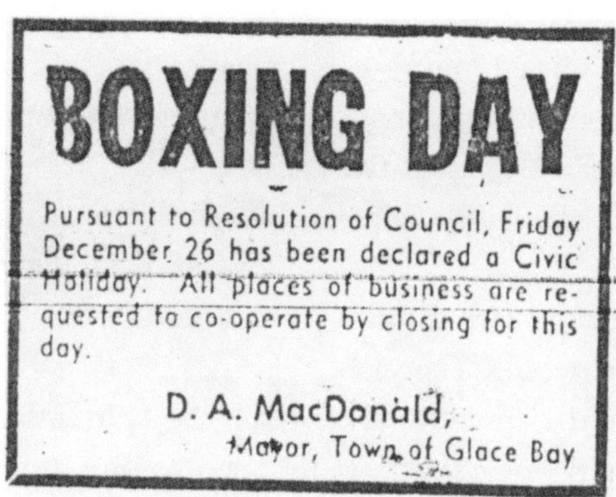

BOXING DAY

Pursuant to Resolution of Council, Friday December 26 has been declared a Civic Holiday. All places of business are requested to co-operate by closing for this day.

D. A. MacDonald,
Mayor, Town of Glace Bay

KWANZAA

DECEMBER 26

DECEMBER 26 IS ALSO THE BEGINNING of a relatively new holiday and one of the few celebrated today whose originator is still living. It is called Kwanzaa and although it began primarily as a holiday to celebrate the culture and heritage of peoples of African decent in the United States, it is the most rapidly assimilated holiday in North America.

Kwanzaa was founded in 1966 by Dr. Maulana Karenga with the hope of educating his people about the African-American struggles and their rich cultural heritage. The holiday lasts for seven days beginning on December 26. It binds the African harvest customs and the social history of African North Americans.

The word Kwanzaa is derived from the East African Swahili phrase "*Mantunde ya kwanza*" which means "the first fruits." The second "a" was added to give the word seven letters which corresponds to the seven symbols, the seven principles and the seven days of Kwanzaa. For this celebration, families and friends gather at meal time. The unity cup is passed from person to person with each one saying something positive about the African-American community. Next, the candles of the kinara are lit and the principles are recited. Everyone talks and dances as the family joins together to rejoice in their heritage.

The celebration is organized around five fundamental activities: ingathering of the people, a special reverence for the Creator and creation, commemoration of the past, re-commitment to one's highest ideals, and celebration of the good around and within each person.

Each day of Kwanzaa concentrates on one of these principles.

December 26, **Umoha** (Unity)—to strive for togetherness both within the family and in the community, nation and race.

December 27, **Kujichagulia** (Self Determination)—to develop one's own identity and pattern one's life after one's self.

December 28, **Ujima** (Collective Work and Responsibility)—working together on matters of common interest.

December 29, **Ujamma** (Cooperative Economics)—to build and maintain an economic base and to profit from it together.

December 30, **Nia** (Purpose)—to build and develop a national community to restore the people to their traditional greatness.

December 31, **Kuumba** (Creativity)—to work toward making one's community more beautiful and beneficial.

January 1, **Imani** (Faith)—to believe in one's self as a people, and the righteousness and victory of the people's struggle.

Kwanzaa has seven basic symbols and two supplemental ones.

Mkeka—a woven mat, symbolic of Black history, the foundation on which all else is built. Typically the other symbols are place upon the mkeka.

Mazao—the crops symbolic of the harvest and rewards for productive and collective labour.

Muhindi—ears of corn, representing children, one ear of corn for each child in the family.

Kinara—a candleholder, symbol of the roots in Africa.

Mishumaa Saba—the seven candles, representing the seven principles of Kwanzaa. Three red candles are place on the left of the kinara representing the struggle; the middle candle is black, representing all people; and three green candles on the right represent the future.

Kikombe cha Umoja—a unity cup, symbolic of staying together

Zawad—gifts, symbolic of the labour and love of parents and the commitments made and kept by the children.

Many people of African heritage in Nova Scotia have added Kwanzaa celebrations to their family traditions. When one looks at the principles advocated, it might be a good holiday for us all to acknowledge.

NEW YEAR'S EVE DECEMBER 31

ALTHOUGH NEW YEAR'S EVE is not properly considered a holiday, for many people, it is one of the most anticipated and celebratory calendar events. It is the last day in the calendar, an opportunity to reflect upon the past year and make plans for the future. We can begin anew and, while many New Year's resolutions are made, few are honoured!

Celebrations vary around the world and some of the icons we associate with New Year's celebrations are ancient. The tradition of using a baby to signify the New Year began in Greece around 600 BC. The beginning of the Greek New Year was also a time to celebrate Dionysus, the god of wine, by parading a baby in a basket. The baby represented the annual rebirth of Dionysus as the spirit of fertility. And if the New Year was to be represented by a newborn, the dying year would naturally be symbolized by an old man. The image of a baby with a dated banner as a symbolic representation of the incoming new year was brought to North America by early German settlers. They had used the effigy since the fourteenth century.

The Scottish New Year's celebration of Hogmanay is not so old. It probably evolved in the sixteenth century and it is certain that elements from this celebra-

The last of the Old Year.--Tearing Down the Seven.

tion were brought to Nova Scotia by the early Scots. The etymology of the word "Hogmanay" has been debated, and several possible sources have been cited. It is said to have come from the Anglo-Saxon *Haleg Monath* (Holy Month); the Gaelic *oge maidne* (New Morning); a Flemish combination of *hoog* (high or great), min (love or affection) and *dag* (day); and finally the Norman French word *hoguinané* (gift at New Year).

What is clear are the customs associated with Hogmanay that are also common to our own celebrations. All debts should be paid, any borrowed items returned, clothes mended, and instruments tuned. At midnight, Hogmanay participants join hands and sing *Auld Lang Syne*.

Many Nova Scotian families follow similar customs. Some people not only insist on having their bills paid off but always see in the New Year with a supply of money in the house. This is said to ensure prosperity for the coming year. One friend told me how she and the other female members of her family put paper money outside the threshold of their door and, at the stroke of midnight, sweep it into the house! She calls it "sweeping in the New Year."

The observances held by our Nova Scotian ancestors had, at least on the outside, less monetary interests. They were more concerned with the soul. Folklore collector Arthur Fauset was told that in the nineteenth century, Nova Scotia Methodists would hold "watch meetings" on New Year's Eve. The faithful were supposed to "watch" for the New Year and believed they should be on their knees when the New Year arrived—at prayer from one year into the next. Many families of Scottish heritage held watch night services on *Oidche Ch'oinnie* (New Year's Eve) in the Presbyterian churches. Then they would all go home to an Open House. There, the oldest person in the assembly would pour drinks after which a whole cake was brought forth as a symbol of hospitality. The second oldest cut the cake, which was served by the youngest.

In Antigonish County, it wasn't just the people who got the treats; the oxen, cattle, hogs, and poultry received extra grain. Then before midnight, every window in the house was lit with candles and the doors were locked. A company of men from the district visited each house. They knocked on the door with their *caman* (clubs) and the man of the house cried out, "Gabh do dh'uan," to which the outside leader replied with a verse or two of a New Year's poem (Duan Callain). Then the doors were opened and whiskey and other refreshments were served.

New Year's was a time to gather with family and renew the bonds of kinship. An original composition by the Reverend Malcolm Campbell titled "Òran Na Bliadha Ùire" (New Year Song) is found in *Gaelic Songs in Nova Scotia* by Helen Creighton and Calum MacLeod. Dr. Creighton collected it from Mr. R. B. MacLeod, Briton Cove, Cape Breton. It was written for the author's mother, telling her how much he missed her. The first verse, which makes reference to the New Year is:

O'n tha bhliadhna so aig deireadh,
'S Bliadhn' Ùr eile nise làimh ruinn;
'S còir gun sgriobh mi beagan fhacail
Do'n té dh'altrum mi 'n a m'phàisde.

(Since this year is at an end, and another New Year is now approaching; it is fitting that I write you a few words in praise of the woman who nursed me when a child.)

In Pictou County the Scottish settlers held balls on New Year's Eve. Favourite tunes were: "Lord MacDonald's Reel," "Flowers of Edinburgh" and "Roy's Wife." New Year's balls and dances are still very popular. Its one of the few times people pull out all the stops, get dressed to the nines and literally ring in the new year with bells, whistles, and other noise makers.

No doubt the ancient belief associated with this custom was to scare the bad forces away. According to Arthur Fauset, who did the majority of his folklore research in the southern end of Nova Scotia, anyone could go into the church on New Year's Eve and ring the bells. Sometimes crowds of boys would travel from church to church. In many communities special fires were lighted to welcome the New Year. On New Year's Eve in 1801, Alexander Stewart kindled one such fire on Mount Thom.

A third tradition common throughout the province was "firing in the New Year." The 1861 diary of Adolphus Gaetz, a merchant in Lunenburg, tells of boys and men from the town firing in the New Year

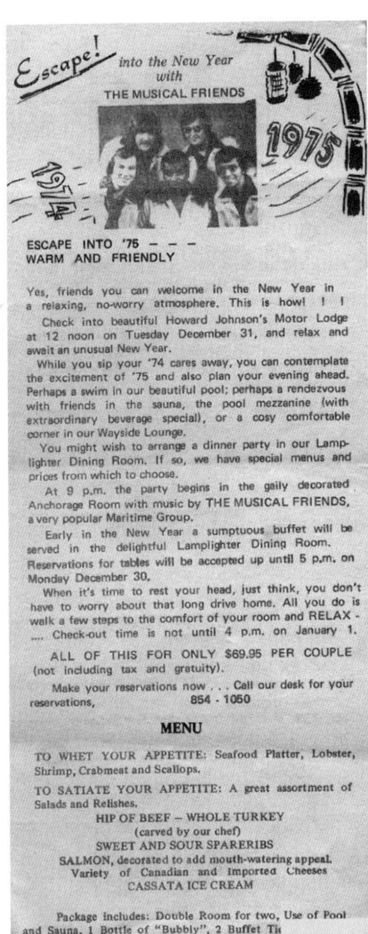

Clary Croft and the Musical Friends, New Year's Eve ad for Howard Johnson's Motor Lodge, Moncton, 1975.

while the bells of the Lutheran Church tolled it out. At Whynacht's Settlement, New Year's Eve was called Old Year's Night. People would come to your door and call out in German, "Can you fire?" Depending on their wishes, those inside would answer yes or no. One of Helen Creighton's most useful German sources from Lunenburg County was Danny Slauenwhite, who recited a rhyme for shooting in the New Year in German and pseudo-German phonetics. The approximate English translation is:

I wish you a happy New Year,
We stand now on your ground,
Our guns and pistols we got ready to fire;
If you don't want us to fire, tell us,
But you are satisfied for us to fire
So we let it crack.

This was also the time when some of the Lunenburg belsnicklers were winding up their celebrations—oftentimes by firing in the New Year. Helen Creighton was told of a time when some belsnicklers went out drinking and then decided to attend the watch night service. They entered the church reverently, but forgot and brought in their guns. The minister saw them and said, "Tut, tut, tut, tut, tut, I dismiss the service."

Firing in the New Year is still celebrated in many communities in Nova Scotia. While it is often done with fireworks, there are still people who will discharge a shotgun into the night sky. While they are merely following a New Year's ritual once celebrated by their ancestors, it can sometimes bring unwanted consequences. In the early 1950s, when my parents were celebrating their first New Year's Eve in their newly-constructed home in Sherbrooke, my dad went to the back doorstep at midnight and fired off his shotgun. Next morning, he discovered he had shot down the clothesline.

Another tradition from my family, and one I rarely find today, is the custom of hanging up a stocking on New Year's Eve. We were always told it was Mrs. Claus who came to fill it, usually with candy, nuts and fruit, and perhaps, a small toy or colouring book. One woman told me she knew of the same tradition in New Brunswick, except the one bringing the gifts was known as Nancy Xmas. Marion Robertson writes of a similar tradition among some families in Shelburne County, where New Year's Eve was known as Old Christmas and the stockings were filled by Kris Kringle, Santa Claus's brother. They had nuts, figs, dates, and money in the toe, for a prosperous year ahead. A friend told me of a tradition in their family at Port Hawksbury, where they would hang up their mittens and find them filled with treats and money.

After midnight on New Year's look in the mirror and you will see the man you are going to marry. (Creighton)

If a baby is born on New Year's Eve near midnight, don't dress it in white. (Creighton)

DECEMBER 31

We no longer hang our stockings for Mrs. Claus in my family (although I did reinstate the custom for my wife last Christmas—her first New Year's Eve stocking!). That's the way custom and tradition goes: it changes and alters with each generation. Holidays have come and gone. Some have been almost completely forgotten while others have turned into huge commercial monsters.

Each of us celebrates in the way we have been taught and then we retain what we want, alter things to suit our changing life styles, or merge our own traditions with those of others. There is one thing we can all be sure of: nothing remains the same.

I hope this book has sparked some memories for you. I also hope you have come to understand and appreciate some of the holiday traditions and cultural beliefs not associated with your own heritage. But, most of all, I wish you Happy Holidays!

NON-WESTERN HOLIDAYS

NON-WESTERN HOLIDAYS

THE GOVERNMENT OF NOVA SCOTIA follows the Gregorian or Christian calendar. Christianity, whose adherents make up approximately one third of the world's people, is currently the religion with the largest number of followers worldwide.

The Gregorian calendar is the one most used by world businesses and governments. It's based on a solar calendar system, and requires modification through slight time changes and leap years to make accurate adjustments. The calendar year begins in January, unlike many non-Gregorian calendars.

When holidays follow lunar, solar, or a combination of both to mark time, it's impossible to accurately put those celebrations into a calendar date. Books of days and calendars will frequently list them in the current month they fall in, but over time even that method will need adjusting.

The holidays listed in this book are, for the most part, based upon days celebrated according to invented popular custom, civic rule or religious beliefs. The major religions found in Nova Scotia, and ranked according to statistics published by The United Nations for the number of adherents in the world, are as follows: Christianity, Islam, Hinduism, Buddhism, Sikhism, Judaism, Baha'i, and Wicca.

Of course, this list doesn't reflect the Mi'kmaq's pre-contact spiritual beliefs.

MI'KMAQ

THE PRE-CONTACT MI'KMAQ followed a seasonal and lunar cycle. Their religion was based upon a belief in a supreme being, but also included a number of lesser spiritual beings and cultural heroes. The best known of these heroes is Kluskap (Glooscap). Seasonal cycles (first salmon run, new moon), social endeavors (hunting, political agreements), and rites of passage (birth, marriage and death) were all causes for celebration. The act of ceremony was almost a daily routine. Ceremony was also considered sacred, to be entered into with a pure heart ready to receive the spiritual guidance that came through praying, fasting, singing, and other sacred rituals.

When the French settled in the Mi'kmaw lands, the Jesuit priests introduced the teachings of the Catholic church. Chief Membertou was the first Mi'kmaw to convert to Catholicism at Port Royal in 1610. By the end of the seventeenth century, most Mi'kmaq had accepted or acknowledged some form of Catholicism. By the time Dr. Helen Creighton was conducting her pioneering folklore collecting in Nova Scotia in the twentieth century, it was assumed by collectors and many scholars that most of the old pre-contact ways had disappeared. But many of the old ways and celebrations had merely gone underground, protected by the elders.

However, collectors were able to find material that showed a blending of traditional Mi'kmaw ceremonies and Catholic holidays. In the 1940s and 1950s, Helen Creighton recorded audio material from several singers and storytellers that illustrates a fusion of traditional songs with parts of the rituals the Church, many translated into the Mi'kmaw language. (In 2000, the Helen Creighton Folklore Society began supporting Mi'kmaw elders and tradition-bearers in the translation of these recordings and have plans to publish the findings.) In the 1970s, Mi'kmaw elder Sarah Denny of Eskasoni supervised the publication of the *Micmac Hymnal* for the Micmac Association of Cultural Studies. It contains a number of Mi'kmaw/Christian songs in the Mi'kmaw language for such holidays as Christmas, Lent and St. Anne's Day. (See: July)

While St. Anne's Day is still celebrated by many Mi'kmaq and non-natives alike, another holiday, the festival of St. Aspinquid has almost disappeared. It seems to have reached its primary focus in the

eighteenth century and was described briefly in the *Halifax Gazette* of June, 1770: "On Thursday last, being the 31st day of May, the festival of St. Aspinquid was celebrated at North West Arm at Nathan Ben Saddi Nathan's and at Captain Jordan's, both fishermen, when elegant dinners at both places were provided, consisting of various kinds of fish, etc. After dinner at Mr. Nathan's were discharged a number of cannon, and at Mr. Jordan's, muskets, and many loyal toasts were drunk in honor of the day. At Mr. Jordan's the toasts, after the usual manner, were the twelve sachem chiefs of the twelve tribes, who were general friends and allies of the English."

An important contemporary day for Mi'kmaq and non-natives is held each October 1. It is called Treaty Day and marks the anniversary of the treaty signed in 1752 with the British Government. In 1986, Mi'kmaw Grand Chief Donald Marshall Sr. called upon the Mi'kmaw Nation to "observe October 1, 1986 and every year thereafter as Treaty Day to commemorate the unique and special relationship that exists between the Mi'kmaq and Her Majesty."

In 1996, the Government of Canada proclaimed June 21 as a national day of celebration and reflection on the history and contributions of Aboriginal Peoples in Canada. It is also commonly known as in North America as the National Indian Day of Prayer.

It is traditionally a sacred time marking the summer equinox and the beginning of new growth. In Christian-Native communities it is a day of worship, prayer and fasting.

ISLAM

The world religion with the second highest number of adherents is Islam. Followers of the religion of Islam are called Muslims. The Muslim population in Nova Scotia is growing rapidly. In fact, if current population growths are realized, world population of Muslims is expected to surpass that of Christians by the middle of the twenty-first century. As with other religious and cultural groups whose traditions follow calendar dates other than those prescribed in the Gregorian calendar, Muslims work and conduct interactive activities and business on the same dates as their Western contemporaries. However, for religious and ceremonial events they follow the lunar Islamic or Hijra calendar. The Muslim calendar, which is organized in cycles of thirty years, begins in the Gregorian calendar date of 622 AD, marking the date when Mohammed left Mecca for Medina. The months are named: Muharrem, Saphar, Rabi 1, Rabi 2, Jomad 1, Jomad 2, Rejab, Shaaban, Shawwal, Dulkaada, and Dhul Haj.

Some of the most significant Muslim holidays are:

Al-Hijra/Muharram (New Years)—celebrated on the first day of Muharrem.

Mawlid al-Nabi—the twelfth day of Rabi 1, Mawlid al-Nabi is a celebration of the birthday of the Prophet Muhammad, the founder of Islam.

Ramadan—the holiest period in the Islamic calendar, Ramadan is held during the entire ninth lunar month of the year. This was the month in which the Qura'n was revealed to the Prophet Muhammad. Muslims over the age of twelve are expected to fast and abstain from sex from sunup to sundown.

Id al-Fitr (Breaking of the Fast)—occurs on the first day of the tenth month, which is the day after Ramadan ends. Houses are decorated, gifts are bought for relatives and special gifts or Zakat, which are alms, are given to the needy.

Yom-ul-Haj (Pilgrimage to Mecca)—begins on the ninth day of Dhul Haj. All Muslims have an obligation, if their means and health can sustain it, to undertake at least one Haj during their lifetime.

Id al-Adha—held on the tenth day of Dhul Haj, after the Haj, is called the Feast of Sacrifice. It recalls the day when Abraham intended to comply with God's instructions to sacrifice his son.

HINDUISM

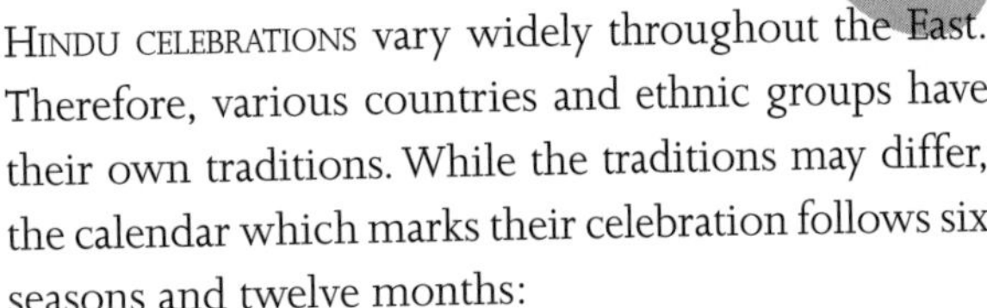

HINDU CELEBRATIONS vary widely throughout the East. Therefore, various countries and ethnic groups have their own traditions. While the traditions may differ, the calendar which marks their celebration follows six seasons and twelve months:

The seasons are:
Vasanta, spring; Grisma, hot season; Varsa, rainy season; Sarad, autumn; Hemanta, winter; and Sisira, frost season.

The months are:
Chaitra, March/April; Vaisaka, April/May; Jyaistha, May/June; Asadha, June/July; Sravana, July/August; Bhadrapada, August/September; Asvina, September/October; Karttika, October/November; Margasira, November/December; Pausa, December/January; and Magha, January/February.

Some important Hindu celebrations are:

Ramnavami—the anniversary of the birth of Lord Rama who was an incarnation of Vishnu. It is celebrated on the ninth day of Chaitraq. Ramnavami is a time to reflect on one's duties and responsibilities toward others.

Holi—a spring festival celebrated in Chaitraq. It is a joyous celebration commemorating the burning of Holika, an evil being who tormented people all over India. Naturally, bonfires are popular. It is dedicated to Krishna or Kama, the God of Pleasure.

Diwali (Row of Lights)—a five day festival held in Asvina or Karttika. It is considered the Hindu New Year. The festival celebrations begin with a cleansing of homes and people and new clothes are put on. Prayers are said at temples and in homes. Fireworks and decorating with strings of lamps or other lights are part of the celebrations. Many Hindus now send Diwali cards, similar to ones with good wishes sent by Christians at Christmas.

BUDDHISM

There are three main schools of Buddhism: Asian, Tibetan, and Chinese (which can also include Korean, Japanese and Vietnamese). Buddhists have diverse regional traditions and holidays which are celebrated by many different ethnic subgroups. In most areas of the world, the holy days are synchronized with the phases of the moon. They include:

Nirvana Day—held in mid-February. It commemorates the death of Siddhartha Gautama, the Buddha.

Wesak (Vaisaka)—the fourth moon of the lunar calendar, Wesak is Buddha's birthday. It is considered the most important day of the year for Buddhists. In some traditions, it celebrates the Buddha's birth, enlightenment and death.

Bodhi Day—celebrated in early December, Bodhi Day recalls the Buddha's enlightenment in BC 596.

Nova Scotia is now a world-recognized centre for Buddhism. It began in 1977 when Chogyam Trungpa, Rinpoche, a Tibetan Buddhist leader, first came to Nova Scotia believing it was the right place to live and continue his spiritual work. He eventually moved here in 1979 and encouraged many of his students to move from Colourado and elsewhere. Buddhists in Nova Scotia have added to and altered the mainstream cultural and commercial activities of the province, but have not made attempts to proselytize. Still, many Nova Scotians have begun to follow the form of meditation practice taught at the Shambhala Training Centre in Halifax.

While many Nova Scotian Buddhists mark the important Buddhist holidays, they also celebrate the traditional holidays that were part of their Western upbringing. Most first-generation Buddhists in Nova Scotia became practitioners in their adulthood. However, since the 1970s we have seen a second generation of Nova Scotians merging their Buddhist teachings with those of their parents and non-Buddhist contemporaries. As of yet, no traditional Buddhist holidays have entered the popular folk idiom in Nova Scotia, and it will be interesting to see if Nova Scotians will one day be celebrating a Buddhist holiday as the general population does Easter, with its mix of religious and secular traditions.

SIKHISM

Much has been learned and written about the influence of the Sikh community in Canada, especially in British Columbia. Sikhs in Nova Scotia, like those over the world, celebrate the birthdays of their ten gurus, the spiritual teachers of Sikhism. Two of these leaders in particular are celebrated with holidays which I have transposed to the Gregorian calendar:

Birthday of Guru Nanak—on a prescribed day close to the end of November, the birth of Guru Nanak, the first guru is celebrated. He is said to have founded the Sikh faith and taught that there was neither Muslim nor Hindu. The book of scriptures (Guru Granth) is read for two days and two nights after which a communal meal is served.

Birthday of Guru Gobind Singh—sometime between December and January, a celebration to honour the birth of Guru Gobind Singh, the tenth and last of the gurus. He was responsible for reorganizing Sikhism and he also founded the Khalsa brotherhood.

In addition to these two important events, Sikhs have a number of other holy days:

Holi (a festival shared with Hinduism)—is a celebration of spring where people light bonfires and make music.

Baisakhi Day—is also shared with Hinduism. Originally a harvest festival, it is held on the anniversary of the date in 1699 when Guru Gobind Singh founded the Khalsa brotherhood. It is a time of both celebration and worship. The Sikh calendar year begins on this date.

Martyrdom of Guru Arjun Dev—Guru Arjun Dey was the fifth guru and the first martyr of Sikhism. The Mughal emperor Jehangir executed Guru Arjun Dev in mid-May of 1606 by forcing him to sit upon hot irons while burning sand was poured over him. In commemoration of his death, visitors are offered sweetened milk and cool drinks as symbols of cooling the spirits of the oppressed.

Martyrdom of Guru Teg Bahadur—Guru Teg Bahadur was the ninth guru, and another martyr who was executed by the Mughal emperor. He promoted religious freedom.

JUDAISM

ASIDE FROM MIGRANT JEWISH traders and soldiers, the first known Jewish settlers arrived in Nova Scotia at Halifax in1750. They were Isaac Solomon, his Christian wife, Sarah, and their two daughters. By 1752 the records show thirty people—a large enough percentage of the total population of approximately two hundred, to warrant the establishment of a Jewish cemetery on Spring Garden Road. Soon Jewish families were living in Cape Breton and elsewhere, although their activities weren't always documented in the official records. It may be that between 1824 and 1870, no inhabitants were living openly as Jews in the province. The 1871 national census lists no Jews, while the Nova Scotia census for the same year lists thirty. After the 1870s, more Jewish immigration to Nova Scotia took place and rose markedly in the 1920s.

Since Nova Scotian Jews were isolated from mainstream Christian society, and because of anti-Semitism and misunderstanding, they celebrated their holidays in private. Only in the last few decades have multicultural and ecumenical events opened the way for non-Jews to understand and participate in some of the Jewish holiday rituals. And, as in other faiths, the youth have introduced new ways of celebrating the old holidays. In an 1980 issue of *Ha'Ezor—Young Judaea's Regional Newsletter*, published in Halifax by Atlantic Young Judaea, we find an announcement for an upcoming Hanukkah (Chanukah) brunch and find out about future plans for a Purim party and an Israeli Disco.

The Jewish calendar is lunisolar, meaning that the months are determined by the position of the moon and the years by the sun. Each month begins when the new moon first appears, and each day is calculated from sunset to sunset. The calendar begins with the creation of the world.

The lunar months are:

Nissan	March/April
Iyar	April/May
Sivan	May/June
Tammuz	June/July

Av	July/August
Ellul	August/September
Tishri	September/October
Heshvan	October/November
Kislev	November/December
Tevat	December/January
Shevat	January/February
Ada	February/March.

There are many holidays throughout the year. The most significant are:

Pesah (Passover)—this eight-day festival begins on the fifteenth day of the month of Nissan. It marks the passing over by God of the destruction of the first born of Egypt, the act that convinced the Pharaoh to deliver the Israelites from bondage. During Pesah only unleavened bread (matzo) is eaten. This reminds the people of the quick breads their ancestors had to make in their flight from the Egyptians. On the Pesah Eve the Seder is performed. It is a service of worship where ritual foods are eaten and the story of the Pesah is retold.

Shavout—held on the sixth day of the month of Sivan, Shavout recalls God's revelation of the Torah to the Jewish people. The synagogues are decorated with fruit and flowers. Cheese blintzes and cakes are eaten

.

Sukkoth—a nine-day festival beginning on the fifteenth day of the month of Tishri, Sukkoth is also known as the Feast of Tabernacles. It celebrates God's bounty to his people. Some families build a suhkah, which is a small booth, representing the temporary shelters made by the Israelites fleeing Egypt. In the synagogue, a palm branch, a twig of myrtle and branches of willow are carried in the right hand, while an *ethrog* (citrus fruit) is carried in the left. They are held aloft in all directions to symbolize God's presence in the temple and everywhere.

Rosh Hashanah—held on the first and second days of the month ofTishri, Rosh Hashanah is the Jewish New Year. There follows ten days from Rosh Hashanah to Yom Kippur, the Day of Atonement, as days of fasting and penitence. People go to temple and pray for peace and happiness. The *shofar* (ram's horn) is blown to remind the people to follow God's laws. Sweets, especially apples dipped in honey, are eaten in hopes of a better time ahead.

Yom Kippur—known as the Day of Atonement, Yom Kippur is the most holy of days in the Jewish calendar. Penitence, prayer and fasting are important components of this day. An evening service (Kol Nidre) is held and the fast is broken.

Hanukkah—translated as "dedication," Hanukkah is an eight-day celebration beginning on the twenty-fifth day of the month of Kislev. It recalls an event which took place in 165 BC (in the Gregorian calendar) when the Maccabees triumphed over the Greek forces of Antiocus IV. The celebration is also known as the Festival of Lights. When the Jews entered the temple they found only enough oil to light the lamps to last one day; but the oil miraculously continued burning for eight days. Each family lights an eight-candle holder called a menorah. One candle is lighted on each of the eight days. Traditional foods include potato pancakes called latkes and children play a game with a dreydl (four-sided top) and sing a song which begins with the verse:

I have a little dreydl,
I made it out of clay;
And when it's dry and ready
Then dreydl I shall play.
O, dreydl, dreydl, dreydl,
I made it out of clay;
O dreydl, dreydl, dreydl,
Now dreydl I shall play.

Purim—known as "the Feast of Lots," Purim recalls the story in the Book of Esther of the Jewish victory over the Persian King, Ahasueras. The King's overlord, Haman, demanded that everyone should bow before him. Mordecai refused to do this and was ordered executed. To determine the date of Mordecai's death, Haman used a die known as a purim to cast the date, but Queen Esther and her followers were able to overthrow the tyrant. The celebrations of this day includes costumes and parties. A three-cornered pastry is eaten which represents Haman's hat. Children play with a noisemaker called a gragger and make a noise every time Haman's name is mentioned.

BAHA'I

The Baha'i religion first had a presence in Nova Scotia in 1920, when the first Baha'i in the province, John Redden, moved back to his home in Windsor after having converted to the Baha'i faith. However, Mr. Redden eventually left, and by 1937 there were no known adherents to Baha'i living as permanent residents in the province. Then in 1938, three believers settled in the Halifax area. The first advertised public meeting was held in September 1941 in Halifax, where the majority of Baha'is still live.

Baha'i followers in the Middle East organize their yearly celebrations by a lunar and solar calendar. The Bahai solar calendar is made up of nineteen months, each nineteen days long, with four intercalary days for catching up to the solar equation. In other places of the world, Baha'i holy days are structured into the Gregorian calendar. The following holidays have been listed according to where they fall in that calendar:

Naw-Rúz—an ancient Iranian New Year's Day festival, Naw-Rúz occurs near the spring equinox. It is now a world holiday of the Baha'i faith. If the equinox occurs before sunset, then New Year's Day is celebrated on that day in the Middle East; otherwise it is delayed until the following day. In the rest of the world, it is on March 21.

Ridvan—also known as the Most Great Festival and King of Festivals, Ridvan is celebrated on April 21 and recalls the time in 1863 when Baha'u'llah declared he was the prophet predicted by the Bab. It is the most holy day of the Baha'i year.

Declaration of the Bab—occurring on May 23 each year, the Declaration of the Bab recalls the day in 1844 when the Bab declared that he was the individual to make way for Baha'u'llah, the founder of the Baha'i world faith.

Ascension of Baha'u'llah—celebrated on May 29, this day is the anniversary of Baha'u'llah's death.

Martyrdom of the Bab—commemorated on July 9, this holy day is the date in 1850 when the Bab was executed by a firing squad. Followers abstain from work and commerce on this day.

Baha'i—this day honours the memory of the Bab, born Siyyid'Ali-Muhammed in 1819, and is recognized on October 20.

The Birth of Baha'u'llah—is celebrated on his birthday, November 12.

Day of the Covenant—celebrated on November 26, the Day of the Covenant recognizes the day that Baha'u'llah's son Abdul-Baha became the Centre of the Covenant.

Ascension of Abdu'l-Baha—on November 28, Abdu'l-Baha is remembered and honoured for continuing his father's work and his ministries in the Baha'i faith.

WICCA

WICCA IS THE MOST COMMON, yet least understood, neo-pagan religion in North America. It is derived and partially reconstructed from the pagan religion of the ancient Celts. Today there are thousands of individuals and groups practicing various forms of Wicca and other pagan religions throughout the world.

Although there are many differences, there are also some spiritual practices and philosophies that Wiccans and other pagans tend to have in common. There is a strong bond with nature and a desire to live in harmony with the world and its peoples. Because some Wiccans use the term witch, they are frequently misunderstood by mainstream society. Adherents to the Wiccan religion maintain that they do not perform evil magic and worship no evil spirits.

The Wiccan seasonal days of celebration are called Sabbats. There are a total of eight Sabbats. Four minor Sabbats are celebrated at the spring and fall equinoxes and the summer and winter solstices. Dates are approximate:

Spring Equinox—celebrated on March 21, the Spring Equinox marks the beginning of spring and the time when days and nights are of equal length. This is a festival of new growth.

Summer Solstice—also known as Midsummer, this sabbat falls on June 22, and is a celebration of the longest day of the year and the beginning of summer. It is a festival of sharing and service.

Fall Equinox—also known as Mabon, this festival of thanksgiving is on September 23. It is the main harvest festival of the Wiccan calendar and marks the beginning of autumn.

Winter Solstice—celebrated on December 22, this celebration is also known as Yule and Saturnalia. It commemorates the birth of the new solar year and the beginning of winter.

The four major Sabbats are approximately halfway between an equinox and solstice. The most common names for these celebrations are derived from the

Celtic language. In addition, Wiccans also hold special celebrations at or near the time of each full moon, while some also celebrate the new moons. Dates of the major Sabbats are approximate:

Samhain—this sabbat is the first divider of the Celtic year. It is the Wiccan New Year's Eve, and is celebrated on October 31.

Imbolc—held on or near February 2, Imbolc translates as "in the belly," and is a reference to the season of spring. Imbolc celebrates birth and renewal, and is also the festival of light and fire—a time to welcome the returning warmth of the sun.

Beltane—derived from a Gaelic term meaning Belfire (of the Fire of Bel), the Celtic god of light, Beltane is another divider of the two halves of the Celtic year. It is celebrated on May 1.

Lammas—this celebration of prosperity takes place on August 1, marking the middle of summer and the beginning of the harvest.

CHINESE

CHINESE IMMIGRANTS first came to Nova Scotia in the 1890s. The 1891 census lists five Chinese and by 1901, the census listed 104, mostly living in urban centres. The Exclusion Act of 1923 curtailed Chinese population growth and prevented Chinese women from coming to Canada and joining their husbands. The last half of the twentieth century saw a renewed population growth in the Chinese community, and mixed with the substantial Chinese student population from abroad, the community is currently vital and growing.

Although there are many religions in China, there are certain holidays that are observed by the majority of the people in China, and by Chinese people throughout the world. In the 1950s the majority of Chinese in the Halifax area were Christian. They continued to celebrate certain traditional Chinese holidays, as did the more recent immigrants. Chinese Nova Scotians also celebrated some of the holidays of their neighbours.

The Chinese calendar is a lunar-based system. Celebrations are based on Emperor Han Wu Di's almanac. A complete lunar cycle takes approximately sixty years, so the dates are constantly changing from year to year. The sixty year cycle is divided into twelve segments, each one named after an animal.

Legend says that Lord Buddha called all the animals to him before he departed from earth. Only twelve came, and as a reward, he named the years after them in the order they arrived. People born in these years are said to possess the traits of that animal. Examples of the yearly animal symbolism follows. If your birth date isn't listed, adjust the year either way by twelve.

Rat:	1948, 1960, 1972, 1984, 1996
Ox:	1949, 1961, 1973, 1985, 1997
Tiger:	1950, 1962, 1974, 1986, 1998
Rabbit:	1951, 1963, 1975, 1987, 1999
Dragon:	1952, 1964, 1976, 1988, 2000
Snake:	1953, 1965, 1977, 1989, 2001
Horse:	1954, 1966, 1978, 1990, 2002
Sheep:	1955, 1967, 1979, 1991, 2003
Monkey:	1956, 1968, 1980, 1992, 2004
Rooster:	1957, 1969, 1981, 1993, 2005
Dog:	1958, 1970, 1982, 1994, 2006
Pig:	1959, 1971, 1983, 1995, 2007

CHINESE

The most widely celebrated Chinese holiday is the New Year. Similar celebrations in Japan, Korea and Vietnam are known as the Lunar New Year or the Spring Festival. According to the Gregorian calendar the holiday is held on the first new moon after January 20.

Folk legend tells of a winter's eve when a village in China was ravaged by an evil monster. The following year the monster returned. Before it could happen a third time, the villagers devised a plan to scare the monster away. Red banners were hung everywhere, since the colour red is believed to protect against evil. Firecrackers, drums and gongs were used to create loud noises to scare the monster away. The plan worked and the ensuing celebration lasted several days, with exchanging of gifts, dancing and feasting.

Foods during this holiday hold much symbolism. Red meat is not served and one is careful not to serve or eat from a chipped or cracked plate. Fish is eaten to ensure long life and good fortune. Oranges and tangerines symbolize wealth and good fortune. Nan Gao, the New Year's cake, is always served and it is believed that the higher the cake rises the better the year will be.

Red paper packets with money tucked inside are given out as a symbol of good luck. The amount is usually an even number, because odd numbers are regarded as unlucky. Lions are considered to be good omens and so the Lion Dance is performed to repel demons. In addition, everyone celebrates their birthday and turns one year older.

Chinese money envelope.

BIBLIOGRAPHY

Unpublished Sources

Helen Creighton Collection, Canadian Museum of Civilization.

Helen Creighton Fonds, Nova Scotia Archives and Records Management.

Clary Croft (personal research from 1974 - 2002)

Newspapers and Periodicals

Acadian Recorder (Halifax)

Advertiser (Kentville)

Advertiser (Springhill)

Advocate (Pictou)

Atlantic Advocate

Atlantic Insight

British Colonist (Halifax)

Canadian Geographic Journal

Casket (Antigonish)

Chronicle Herald (Halifax)

Citizen (Truro)

Clarion (New Glasgow)

Courier (Digby)

Daily News (Amherst)

Daily News (Halifax)

Daily Post (Sydney)

Eastern Chronicle (New Glasgow)

Evening Mail (Halifax)

Evening News (Halifax)

Family Herald and Weekly Star

Folklore Studies Association of Canada Journal

Fourth Estate (Halifax)

Free Press (Dartmouth)

Gazette(Amherst)

German-Canadian Yearbook

Herald (Halifax)

Journal of American Folklore

Journal of Education (Province of Nova Scotia)

Le Petit Courrier

Mail (Halifax)

Mail Star (Halifax)

Nova Scotia Gazette

The Nova Scotia Gazette and Weekly Chronicle

Nova Scotian (Halifax)

Post (Sydney)

Presbyterian Witness

South Shore Record (Mahone Bay)

Star Weekly

Transcript (Liverpool)

Weekly Monitor (Bridgetown)

Western Chronicle (Kentville)

BIBLIOGRAPHY

Published Sources

Ackhurst, William. *Report of the Board of School Commissioners for the City of Halifax for the year ending October 31, 1885*. Halifax: William McNab, 1886.

African Genealogy Society, eds., with contributions by Donald Clairmont, Stephen Kimber, Bridglal Pachai and Charles Saunders. *The Spirit of Africville*. Halifax: Formac, 1992.

Barris, Ted and Alex Barris. *Days of Victory: Canadians Remember 1939-1945*. Toronto: Macmillan, 1995.

Bauman, Richard. "Belsnickling in a Nova Scotia Community." *Western Folklore*. 31 (1971).

Belcher's Almanac. Halifax: C.H. Belcher, 1870.

Belcher's Almanac. Halifax: C.H. Belcher, 1895.

Belliveau, J.E. "Tales of Phantoms." *Star Weekly*. (July 2, 1957).

Blakely, Phyllis R. "New Year's in Nova Scotia" *Atlantic Advocate*. 62.5 (January 1972).

Brunvand, Jan Harold. *The Study of American Folklore: An Introduction*, 3rd edition. New York: W.W. Norton & Company, 1986.

Campbell, P. J. MacKenzie. *A Highland Community on the Bras D'Or (Red Island, Richmond County)*. Privately printed, 1963.

Child, Francis James. *The English and Scottish Popular Ballads*. 5 Volumes, Boston: 1882-98.

Chinese Directory, Halifax, Nova Scotia 1952. 2.2 Vancouver: Chinese Publicity Bureau, 1951.

Christian, Roy. *Old English Customs*, Devon: Davis and Charles Limited, 1972.

Cohen, Henning and Tristram Potter Coffin, eds. *The Folklore of American Holidays* third edition. Detroit: Gale, 1999.

Colombo, John Robert, ed. *Colombo's Concise Canadian Quotations*. Hurting Publishers, 1976.

Cormier-Boudreau and Melvin Gallant. *A Taste of Acadie*. Fredericton: Goose Lane, 1991.

Creighton, Helen. "Christmas Remembered." *Halifax*. 2.1 (1979).

———. *Folklore of Lunenburg County, Nova Scotia*. Toronto: McGraw-Hill Ryerson, 1950, 1976.

———. *A Life in Folklore*. Toronto: McGraw-Hill Ryerson, 1975.

———. *Bluenose Magic: Popular Beliefs and Superstitions in Nova Scotia*. Toronto: Ryerson, 1968.

———. *Songs and Ballads from Nova Scotia*. New York: Dover, 1932, 1966.

———. *Maritime Folk Songs*. Toronto: Ryerson Press, 1961.

———. "Old Christmas Customs in Nova Scotia." *Canadian Geographical Journal* . 68.6 (1961).

———. "Songs for Christmas." *Atlantic Advocate*. 50. 4 (1959).

———. "Folklore of Victoria Beach." *Journal of American Folklore*. 63 (1950).

———, and Calum MacLeod. *Gaelic Songs in Nova Scotia*. Ottawa: National Museum Bulletin 117, 1964.

———, and Doreen H. Senior. *Traditional Songs from Nova Scotia*. Toronto: Ryerson, 1950.

Crith, Mamie R. *All About the Months* . New York: Harper and Row, 1966.

Croft, Clary. "Helen Creighton: Collecting the German-based Folklore of Lunenburg County, Nova Scotia." *German-Canadian Yearbook*. 16 (2000).

———. *Helen Creighton: Canada's First Lady of Folkore*, Halifax: Nimbus, 1999.

———. *Chocolates, Tattoos and Mayflowers: Mainstreet Memorabilia from Clary Croft*. Halifax: Nimbus, 1995.

———. "What Band That Sunday Morning?" *Share and Care: The Story of the Nova Scotia Home for Coloured Children*. Halifax: Nimbus Publishing, 1994.

Davis, Stephen A. *The Micmac: People of the Maritimes*. Tantallon: Four East Publications, 1991.

Denys, Nicolas. "Concerning the Ways of the Indians: their customs, dress, methods of hunting and fishing, and their amusements." 1672. Nova Scotia Department of Education, n/d.

Dunkling, Leslie. *A Dictionary of Days*. New York: Facts on File Publications, 1988.

Dunlop, Allan C. "The Levee and other New Year's Festivities." *Nova Scotia Historical Quarterly*. 10. 3-4 (1980).

Encyclopaedia of Music in Canada 2nd ed. Toronto: University of Toronto Press, 1992.

Fauset, Arthur Huff. *Folklore from Nova Scotia*. American Folklore Society. 24 (1931).

Fergusson, Donald A. *Fad Air Falbh As Innse Gall: Beyond the Hebrides*. Halifax: Lawson Graphics Atlantic Limited, 1977.

Fergusson, Charles Bruce. "The Labour Movement in Nova Scotia before Confederation," *Public Archives of Nova Scotia Bulletin*, Number 20, 1964.

Forsey, Eugene. "History of the Labour Movement in Canada." *The Canadian Economy: Selected Readings*. Toronto: The Macmillan Company of Canada Limited, 1961.

Foster, Annie H. & Anne Grierson. *High Days and Holidays in Canada*. Toronto: The Ryerson Press, 1961.

Fowke, Edith. *Folklore of Canada*. Toronto: McClelland and Stewart, 1976.

Franklin, John H. *From Slavery to Freedom: A History of Negro Americans*. New York: Vintage Books, 1969.

Fraser, Mary. *Folklore of Nova Scotia*. Antigonish: Formac, 1975.

Goeb, Jan. *The Maritime Jewish Community*. Halifax: Halifax Jewish Historical Society, 1975.

Gosselin, Leslie A. , ed. *Celebration: A Guide to Religious and National Holidays in A Multicultural Milieu*. Multicultural Association of Nova Scotia, 1986.

Grant, John. "Early Blacks of Nova Scotia." *Nova Scotian Journal of Education*. 5 (Fall 1977).

Grant, Robert. *Robert Burns: Scotia's Immortal Bard*. Halifax, 1884.

Ha'Ezor Young Judaea's Regional Newsletter . Halifax: Atlantic Young Judaea, February 1980.

Hatch, Jane M. *The American Book of Days* third edition. New York: The H.W. Wilson Press, 1978.

Hole, Christina. *Easter and Its Customs*. New York: M. Barrows & Co., 1961.

Hopkins, Anthony. *Songs from the Front & Rear: Canadian Servicemen's Songs of the Second World War*,. Edmonton: Hurtig, 1979.

House of Commons Debates. Volume 137, Number 175, 1st Session, 37th Parliament, Official Report (Hansard), 24 April, 2002.

Huntington, Eleanor. *Special Days*. Sydney: privately printed, n/d.

Hutton, Ronald. *The Stations of the Sun: A History of the Ritual Year in Britain*. Oxford: Oxford University Press, 2000.

BIBLIOGRAPHY

Innis, Harold A. editor. *The Diary of Simeon Perkins 1766-1780.* Toronto: The Champlain Society, 1948.

Jolicoeur, Catherine. *Les Plus Belles Légendes Acadiennes.* Montreal: Stanké, 1981.

Karenga, Maulana. *Kwanzaa: A Celebration of Family, Community and Culture.* Los Angeles: University of Sankore Press, 1998.

Kingsbury, Al. *The Pumpkin King: Howard Dill and the Atlantic Giant.* Hantsport: Lancelot Press, 1992.

Kitz, Janet F. *Shattered City: The Halifax Explosion and the Road to Recovery.* Halifax: Nimbus, 1989.

Knockwood, Noel. "Mythology and Religion of the Micmac People." *Social Services News.* Halifax: Nova Scotia Department of Social Services, 1975.

Labor Journal: History of the Labor Movement. Halifax: 1935.

Lacey, Laurie. *Ethnicity and the German Descendants of Lunenburg County, Nova Scotia.* Ethnic Heritage Series, Volume VII, Halifax: International Education Centre, St. Mary's University, 1982.

———. *Lunenburg County Folklore and Oral History: Project 77.* Ottawa: National Museums of Canada, 1979.

Leach, MacEdward. "Celtic Tales from Cape Breton." *Studies in Folklore in Honor of Stith Thompson.* Edson Richmond, ed. Bloomingdale: Indiana University Press, 1957.

Leach, Maria, ed.*Standard Dictionary of Folklore, Mythology, and Legend* 2 volumes. New York: Funk and Wagnalls, 1949-1950.

Litwicki, Ellen M. *America's Public Holidays, 1865-1920* . Washington: Smithsonian Institute Press, 2000.

Lord, Priscilla Sawyer and Daniel J. Foley. *Easter Garland.* New York: Chilton, 1963.

MacDonald, Margaret Read, ed. *The Folklore of World Holidays.* Detroit: Gale, 1992.

Maestro, Maria Erie. *The Chinese in Nova Scotia: An Overview and a Preliminary Bibliography.* Halifax: School of Library and Information Studies, Dalhousie University, 1992.

Martin, John P. *The Story of Dartmouth.* Dartmouth: privately printed, 1957.

Micmac Hymnal, Micmac Association of Cultural Studies, 1975.

Morris, James Rainstrope. *Sable Island Journals 1801-1804.* Transcribed by Rosalee Stilwell, Sable Island Preservation Trust, 2001.

Morrison, James. *Common Heritage: An Annotated Bibliography of Ethnic Groups in Nova Scotia*, Halifax: Education Centre St. Mary's University, Halifax, 1984.

———. "Ethnic Identity in Nova Scotia" *Your World: International Education Centre Newsletter.* 3.1, (1981).

Newall, Venetia. *An Egg at Easter.* London: Routledge & Kegan Paul, 1971.

Nightingale, Marie. *Out of Old Nova Scotian Kitchens.* Halifax: Petheric Press, 1970.

Parsons, Elsie Clew. "Micmac Notes." *Journal of American Folklore.* 39 (1926).

———. "Micmac Folklore." *Journal of American Folklore.* 38 (1925).

People of Nova Scotia: Perpetual Calendar featuring National, Religious and Family Holidays. Multicultural Association of Nova

Porier, Leonie Comeau. *My Acadian Heritage.* Hantsport: Lancelot Press, 1985.

———. "Along the French Shore, St Mary's Bay ." *Novascotian.* March 16, 1965.

BIBLIOGRAPHY

Poteet, Lewis J. *The Second South Shore Phrase Book*. Hantsport: Lancelot Press, 1985.

———. *The South Shore Phrase Book*. Hantsport: Lancelot Press, 1983.

Pottie, Kaye and Vernon Ellis. *Folksongs of the Maritimes*. Halifax: Formac, 1992.

Rand, Silas T. *Legends of the Micmacs*. .New York and London: Longmans, Green, and Company, 1894.

Rankin, D. J. *A History of the County of Antigonish, Nova Scotia*, Toronto: The Macmillan Company Canada Limited, 1929.

Redman, Stanley R. *Gangways: An Account of the Halifax Riots, 1945*. Hantsport: Lancelot Press, 1983.

Ricker, Darlene A. *L'Sitkuk: The Story of the Bear River Mi'Kmaw Community*. Lockport: Roseway Publishing, 1997.

Robertson, Marion. *The Chestnut Pipe: Folklore of Shelburne County*. Halifax: Nimbus, 1991.

Rowland, Beryl. *Animals with Human Faces*. Knoxville: University of Tennessee, 1973.

Sheppard, Tom. *Historic Queens County, Nova Scotia*. Halifax: Nimbus, 2001.

Shyu, Larry N. *The Chinese: Peoples of the Maritimes*. Halifax: Nimbus, 1997.

Swick, David. *Thunder and Ocean: Shambhala and Buddhism in Nova Scotia*. Lawerencetown Beach: Pottersfield Press, 1996.

Thompson, Sue Ellen. *Holiday Symbols* second edition. Detroit: Omnigraphics, 2001.

Ullman, Christiane. "German Folksongs of Lunenburg County, NS." *German-Canadian Yearbook* 5 (1979).

Weaver, Robert S. *International Holidays*. London: McFarland & Company, 1994.

Whitehead, Ruth Holmes. *Stories from the Six Worlds: Micmac Legends*. Halifax, Nimbus, 1988.

———, and Harold McGee. *The Micmac: How Their Ancestors lived Five Hundred years Ago*. Halifax: Nimbus, 1983.

Williams, Paula C. ed., *Candles of Guidance: The History of the Early Halifax Baha'i Community*. Privately published, 1985.

Wilson, J. H. "The Micmac Festival in Cape Breton." *New England Magazine*. 6 (April 1892).

Wilson, Rex H. *The Dialect of Lunenburg County, Nova Scotia*, University of Michigan, 1958.

IMAGE SOURCES

Image Sources

Acadie Masques, St. Joseph-du-Moine: pages 37, 38

Christmas Daddies: page 119

Croft, Clary: pages 17, 30, 77 (photographer Peter Tenwolde), 84, 107, 116, 118, 120, 142, 160

Dartmouth Heritage Museum: pages 13, 27 (C.F. Bell Fonds), 73, 115 (Halifax *Morning Chronicle*, 1922)

Harper, Jeff: page 25

Kaulbach, Kathy: page 147

Nimbus Publishing: page 87

Nova Scotia Archives and Records Management: pages 6, 8 (*Weekly Monitor* [Bridgetown], 5 Jan. 1921), 10, 11 (*Digby Courier*, 1 Jan. 1953), 26 (*Digby Courier*, 16 Feb. 1953), 28, 31, 32 (*Weekly Monitor* [Bridgetown], 2 Feb. 1921), 35, 36 (*Evening Mail* [Halifax], 14 Mar. 1922), 39, 40 (*Evening Mail* [Halifax], 6 Apr. 1922), 42 (*Evening Mail* [Halifax], 12 Apr. 1922), 49 (photographer J.C.M. Hayward), 51 (*Mail Star* [Halifax], 29 Feb. 1957), 58 (*Eastern Chronicle* [New Glasgow], 11 May 1950), 59 (*Advertiser* [Springhill], 30 May 1900), 62 (*Mail Star* [Halifax], 16 June 1949), 64, 65 (*Weekly Monitor* [Bridgetown], 22 June 1921), 66 (photographer Sydney Payne), 74, 81, 82 (*Labour Journal* [Halifax], 1935), 86 (*Eastern Chronicle* [New Glasgow], 5 Oct. 1950), 90 (*Eastern Chronicle* [New Glasgow], 26 Oct. 1950), 99, 100 (*Evening Mail* [Halifax], 11 Nov. 1922), 101 (Arthur Bloomfield Dawson Fonds), 103 (W.H. Buckley Collection), 108 (*Daily Post* [Sydney], Christmas Edition 1902), 110, 113 (CHNS Collection #57), 125, 137 (*Cape Breton Post*, 23 Dec. 1958), 140 (*Advertiser* [Kentville], 31 Dec. 1897)

Nova Scotia Museum of Natural History: page 69 (photographer Clara Dennis, William Dennis Collection)

Saunders, Gary: page 68

PERSONAL CELEBRATIONS

PERSONAL CELEBRATIONS

DATE ____________________

EVENT ____________________

DATE ____________________

EVENT ____________________

DATE ____________________

EVENT ____________________

DATE ____________________

EVENT ____________________

DATE ____________________

EVENT ____________________

DATE ____________________

EVENT ____________________

PERSONAL CELEBRATIONS

DATE ____________

EVENT ____

____

DATE ____________

EVENT ____

____

DATE ____________

EVENT ____

____

DATE ____________

EVENT ____

____

DATE ____________

EVENT ____

____

DATE ____________

EVENT ____

____

PERSONAL CELEBRATIONS

DATE ______________________

EVENT ______________________

____

DATE ______________________

EVENT ______________________

____

DATE ______________________

EVENT ______________________

____

DATE ______________________

EVENT ______________________

____

DATE ______________________

EVENT ______________________

____

DATE ______________________

EVENT ______________________

____